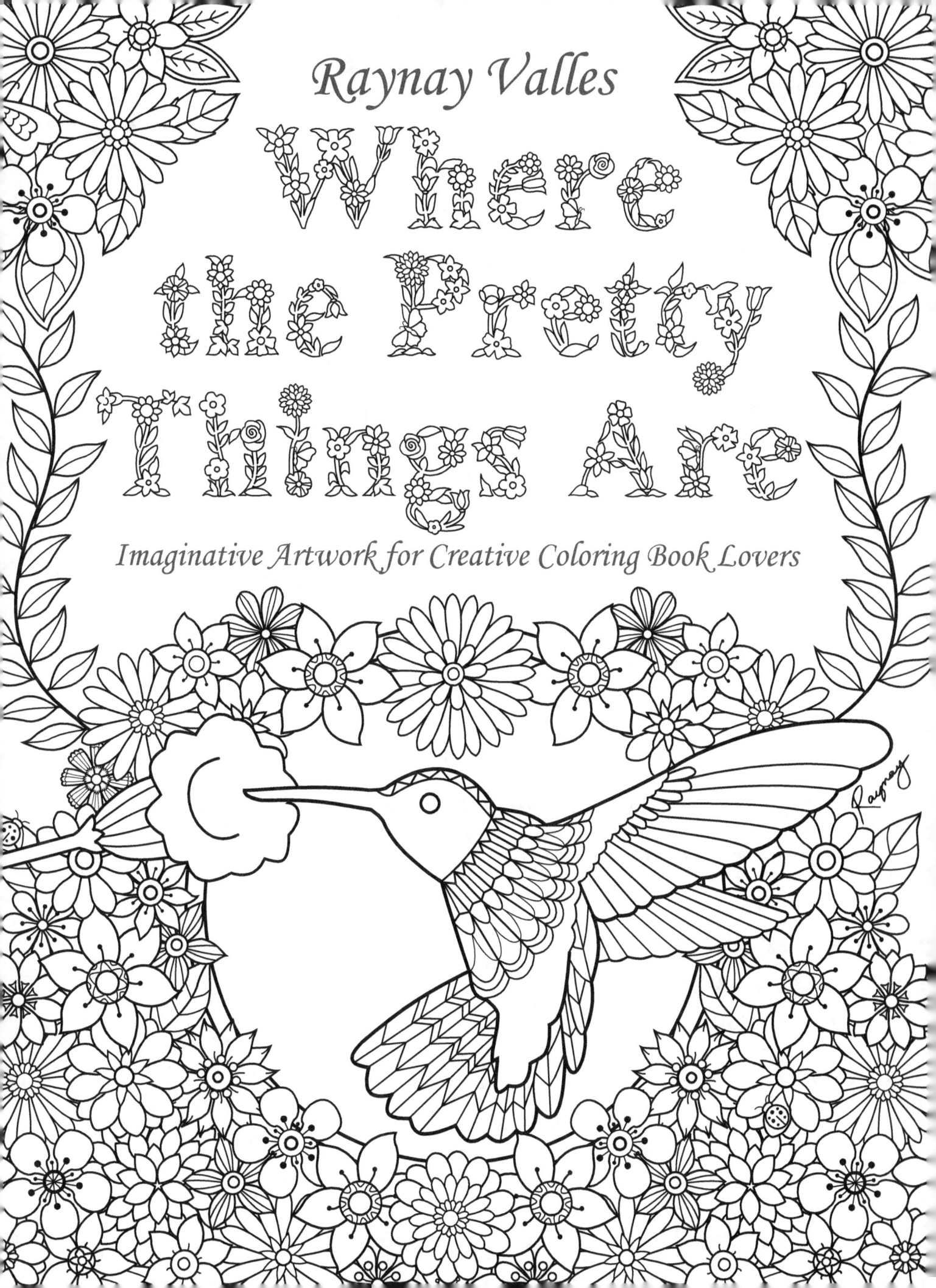

Where the Pretty Things Are

Dedication

This book is dedicated to the unique, creative person holding it.
This book is dedicated to you.

Forward

Inside this book you'll find flights of floral design. Some illustrations grew from seeds in my imagination. Others were inspired by real events, such as finding a stray in our groundcover or neighborhood cats in the backyard.

Coloring is relaxing, creative and fun. Once you're done coloring each page, you'll have a one-of-a-kind piece of art that you can enjoy for a long time.

I had fun creating this collection of drawings. I hope you have fun coloring Where the Pretty Things Are!

Raynay

For stories behind the drawings, visit my website at **www.raynay.com**
Follow me at **www.twitter.com/raynayvalles**
Like my page at www.facebook.com/raynayvallesartist

P.S. You're welcome to show off your colored pages from this book. Put them on the fridge, frame them and mount them on the walls or share them online.

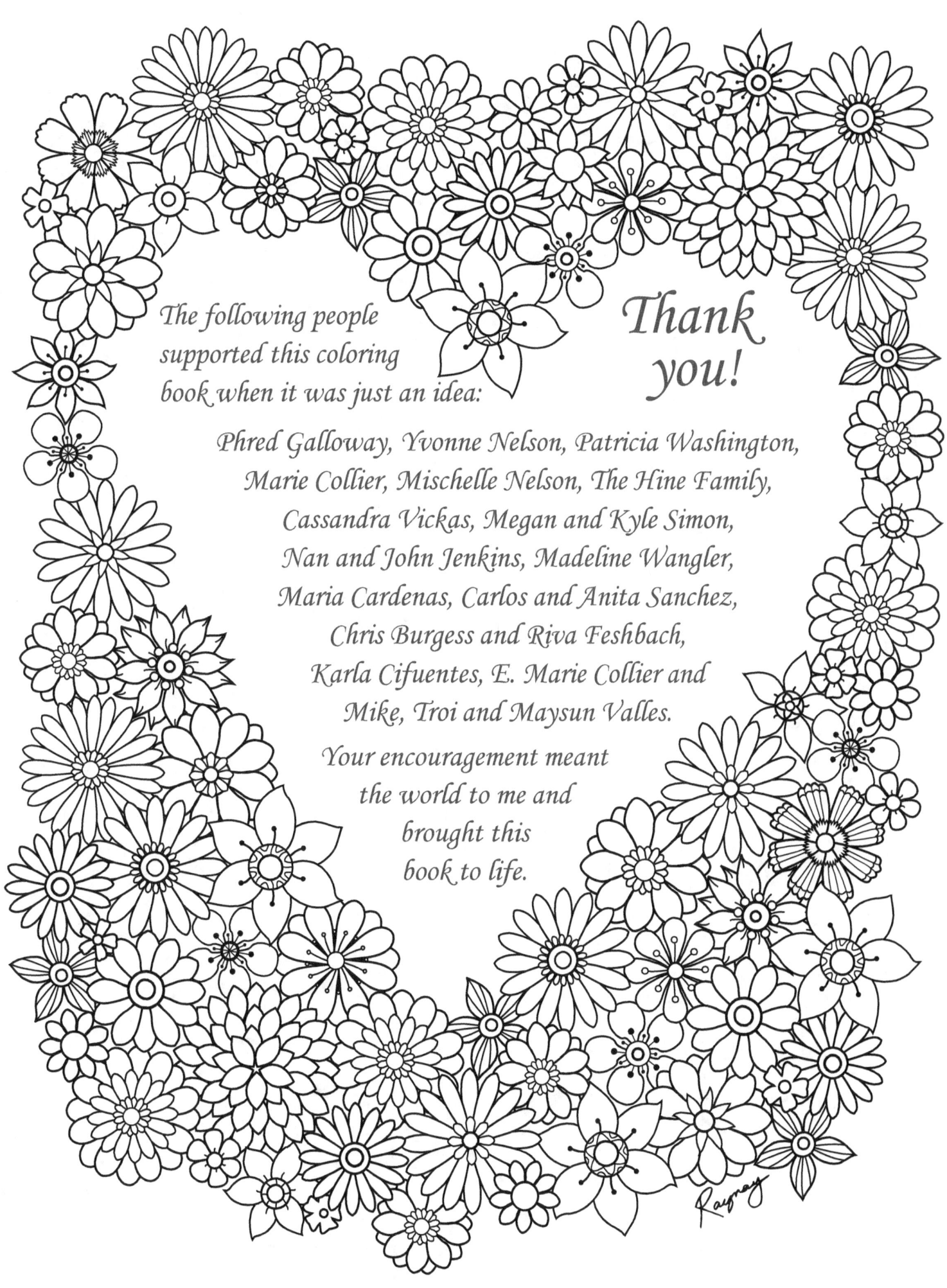

The following people supported this coloring book when it was just an idea:

Phred Galloway, Yvonne Nelson, Patricia Washington, Marie Collier, Mischelle Nelson, The Hine Family, Cassandra Vickas, Megan and Kyle Simon, Nan and John Jenkins, Madeline Wangler, Maria Cardenas, Carlos and Anita Sanchez, Chris Burgess and Riva Feshbach, Karla Cifuentes, E. Marie Collier and Mike, Troi and Maysun Valles.

Thank you!

Your encouragement meant the world to me and brought this book to life.

Title: Gate with Arch

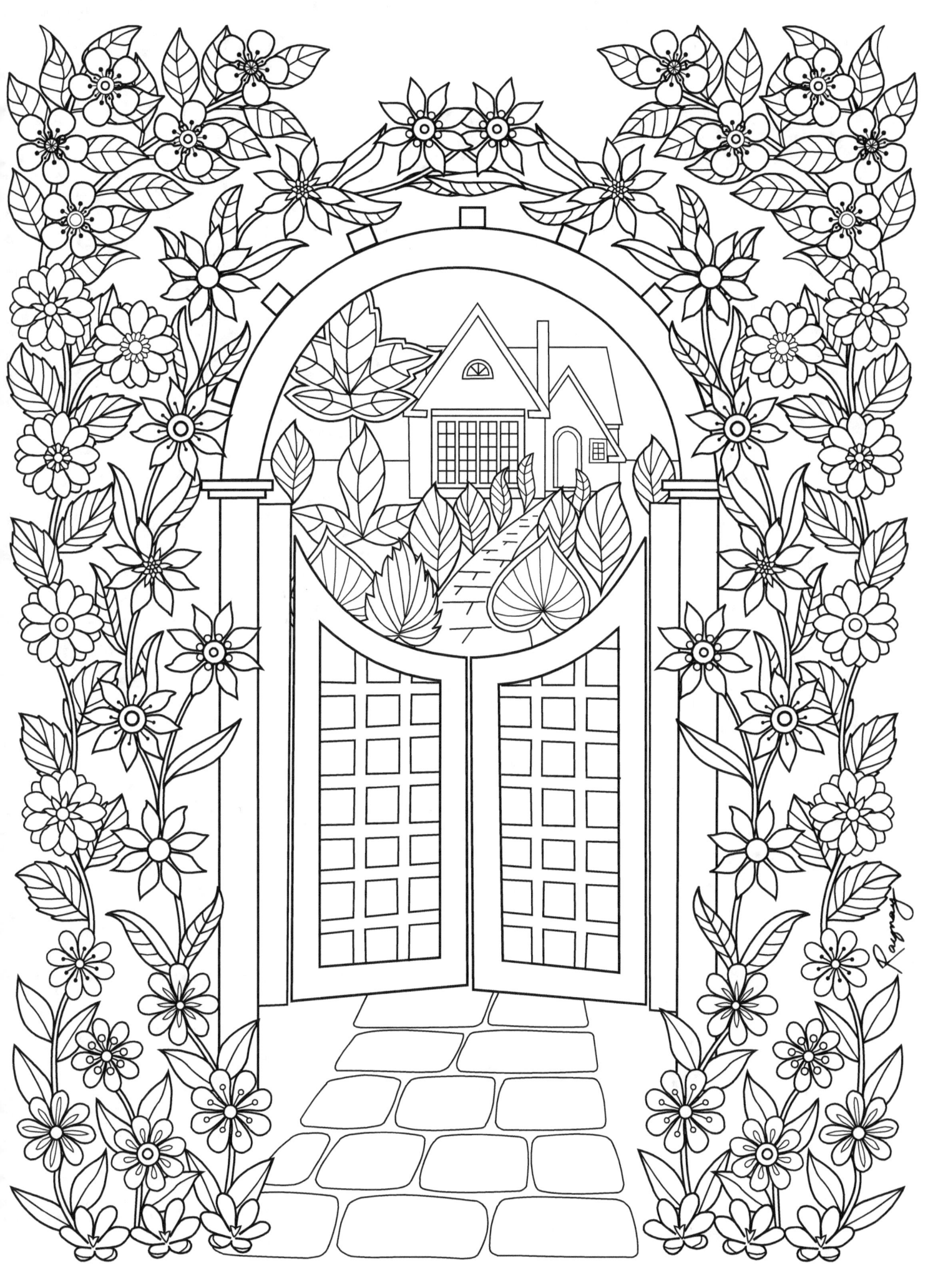

Title: Flower Fireworks

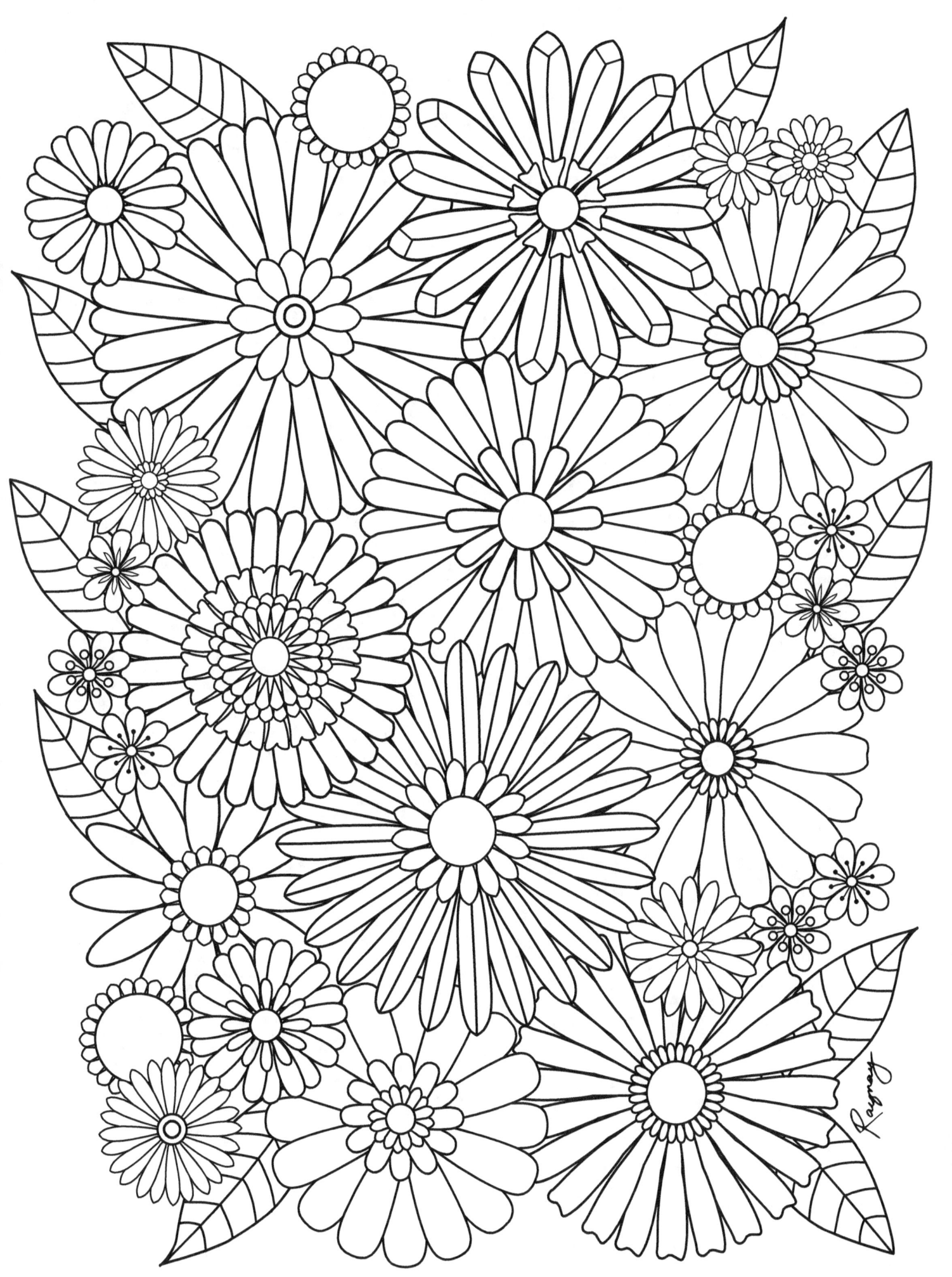

Title: The Peacock

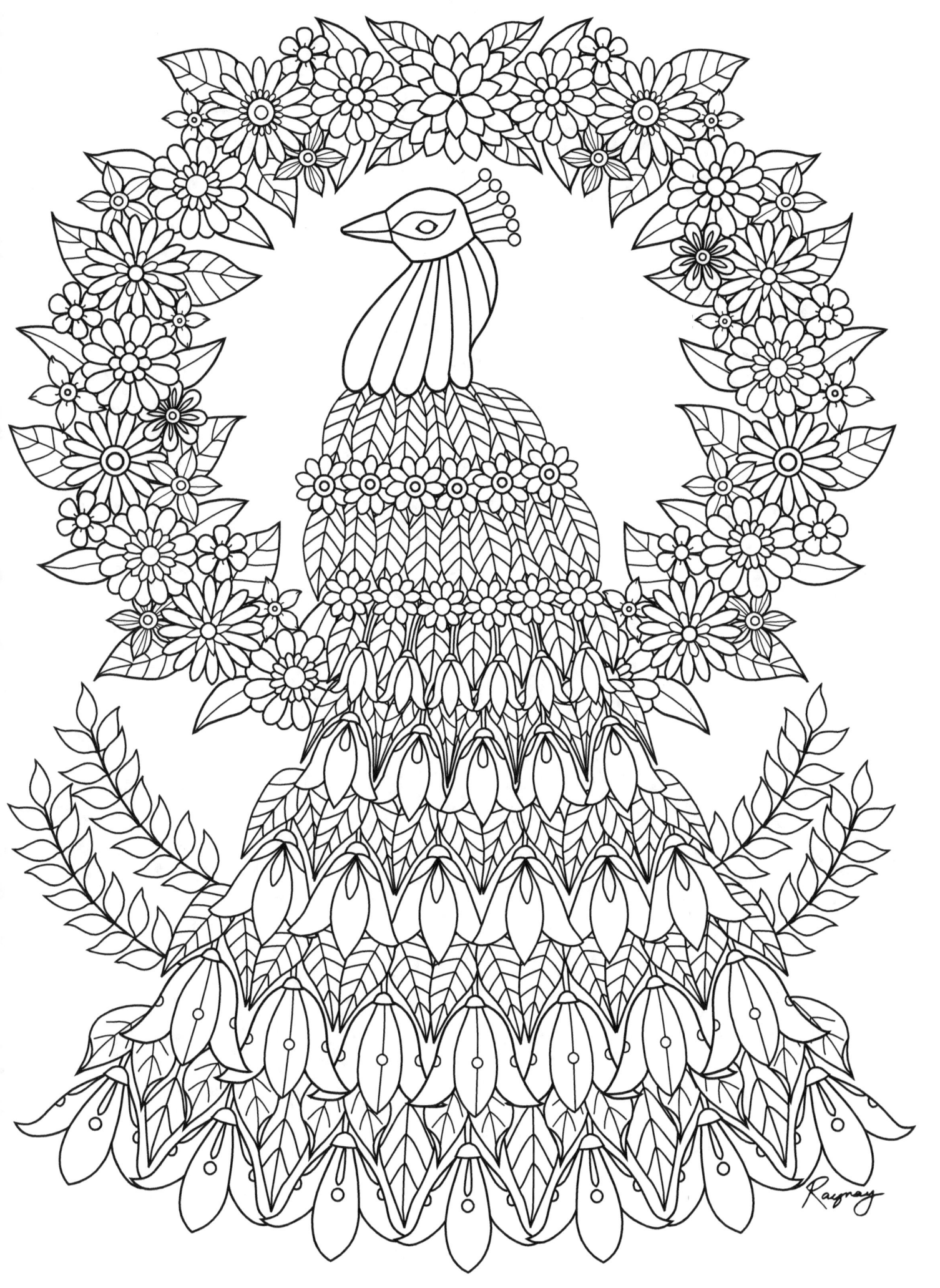

Title: Heart of Flowers

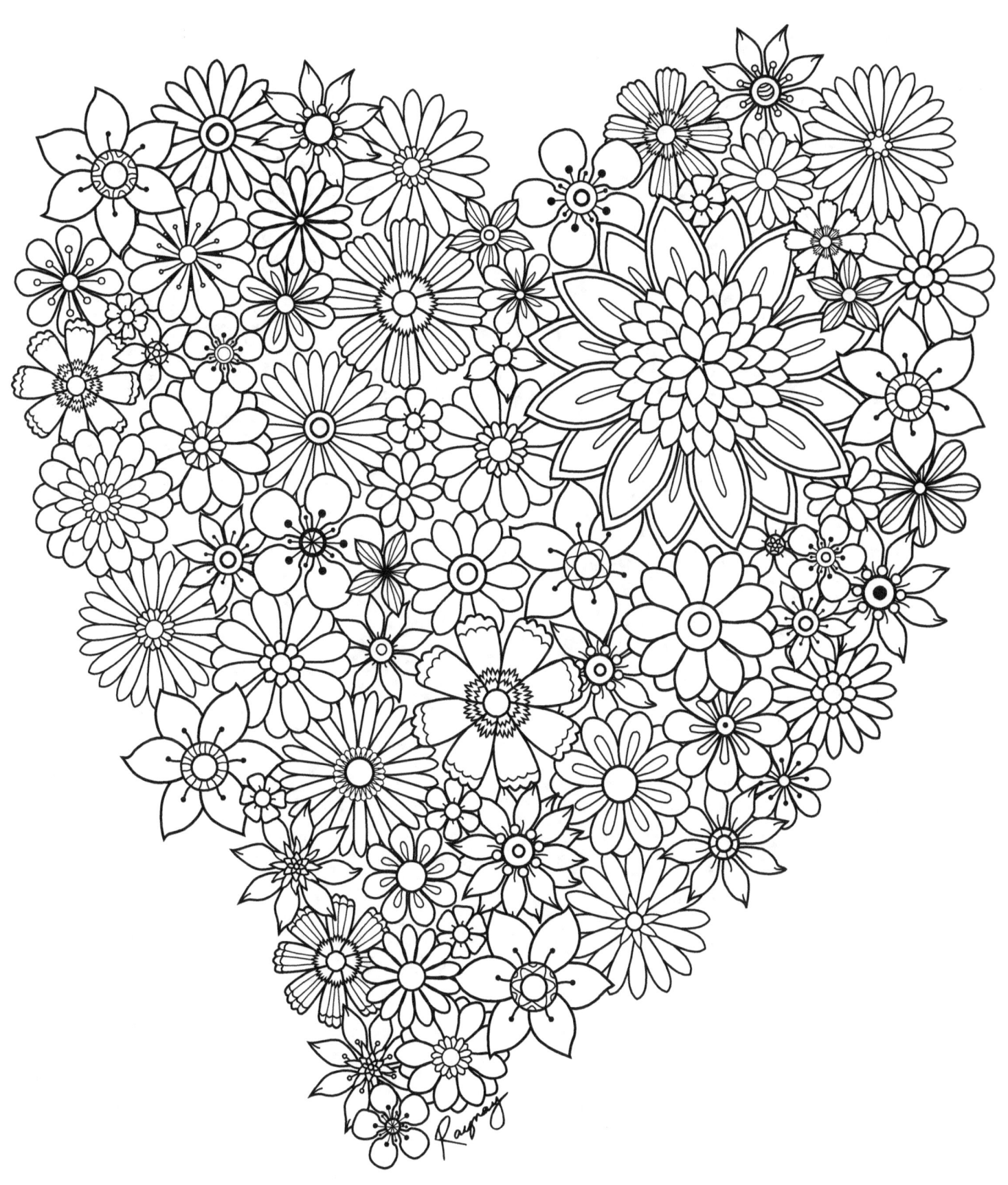

Title: Love of Leaves

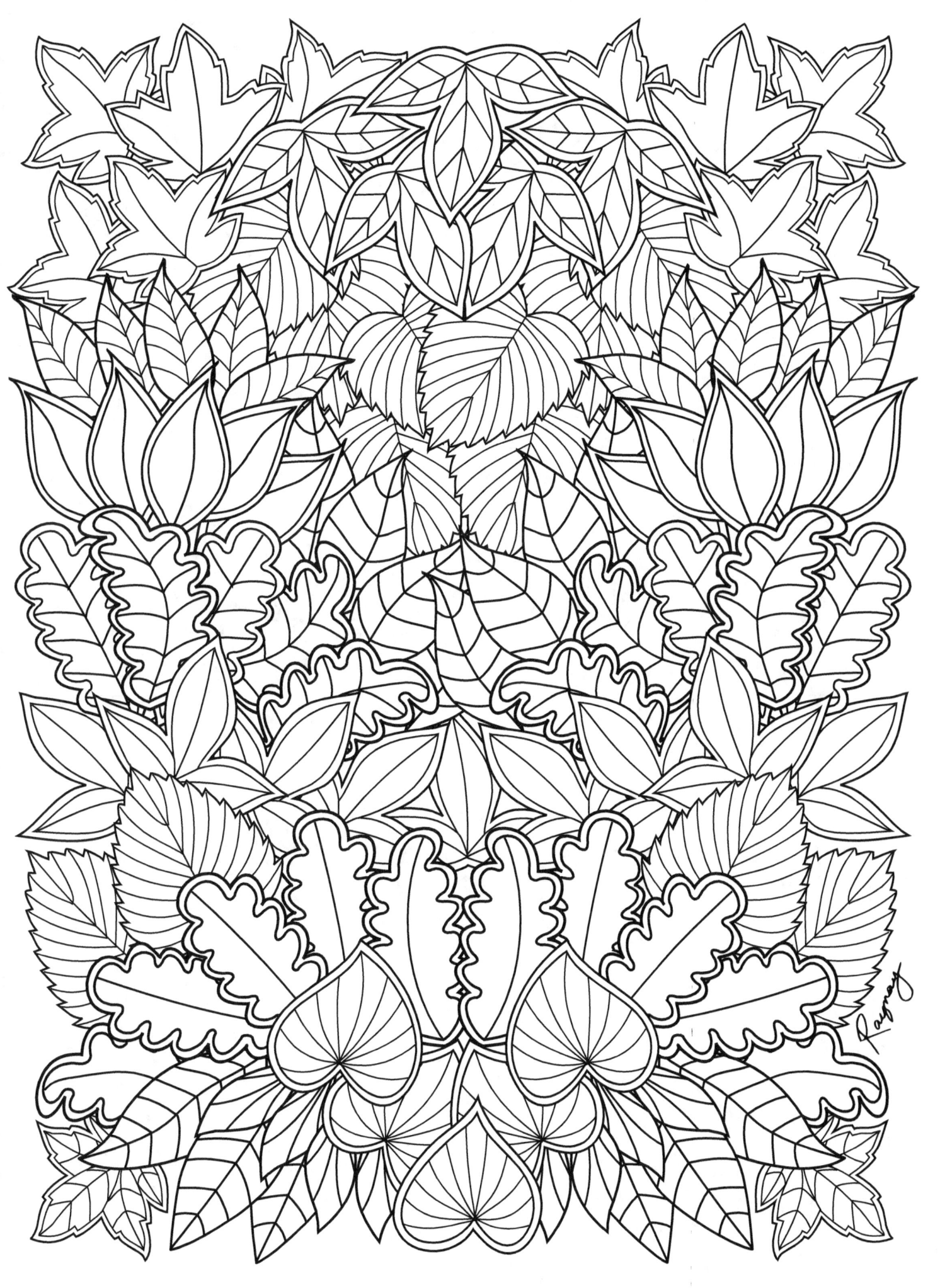

Title: The Floral and Fawn

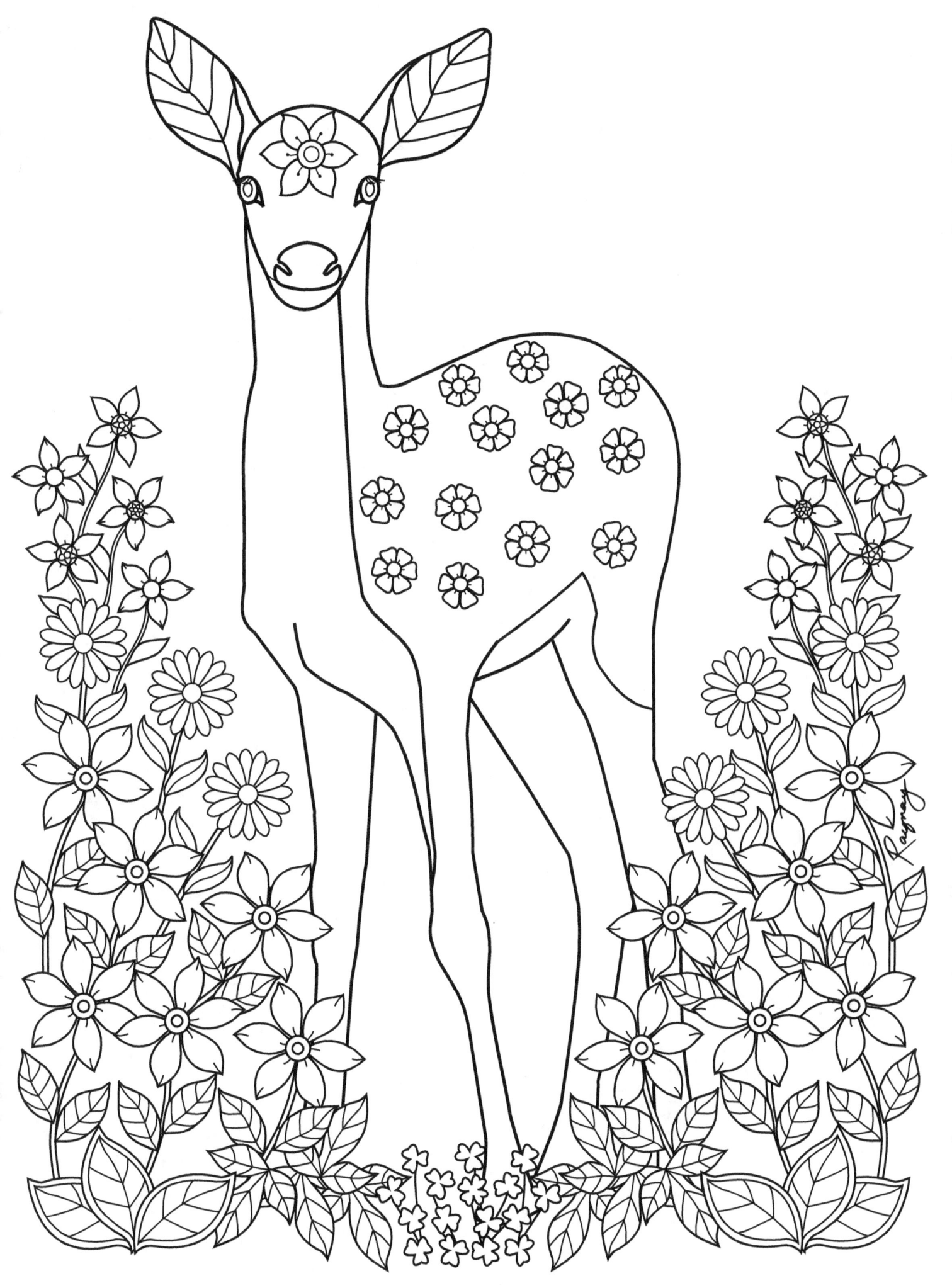

Title: The Lion

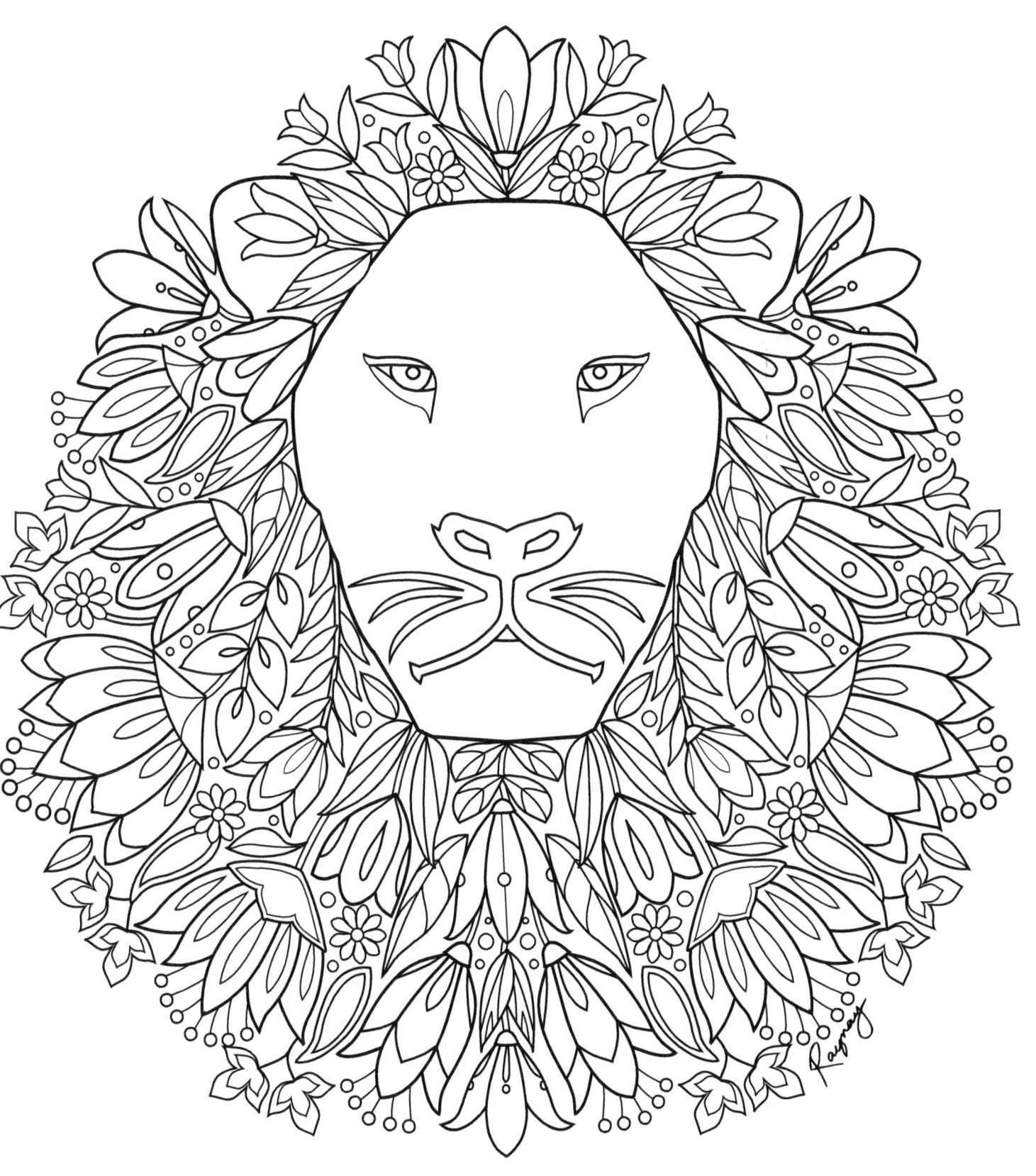

Title: Mailbox Garden

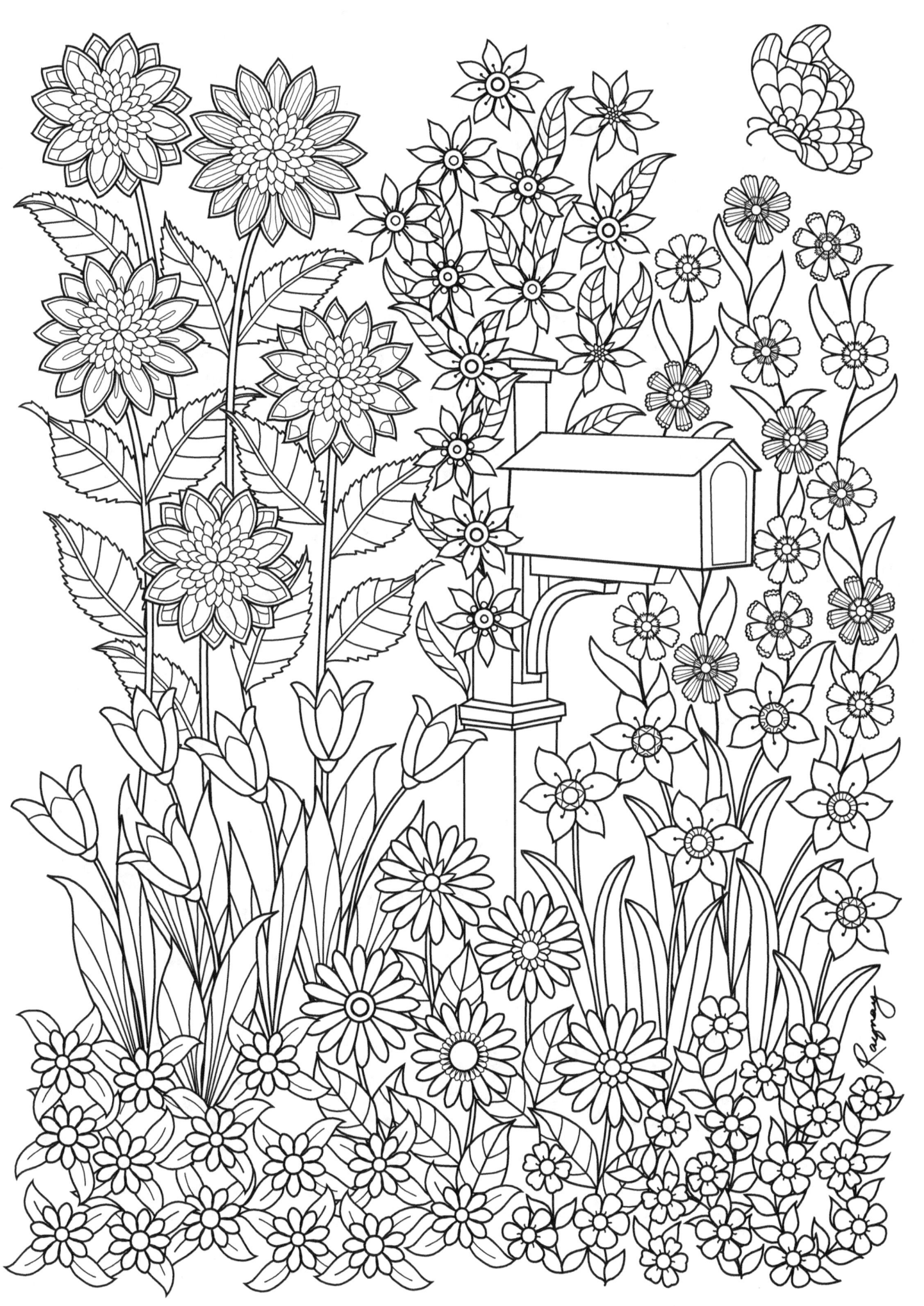

Title: Sunflowers

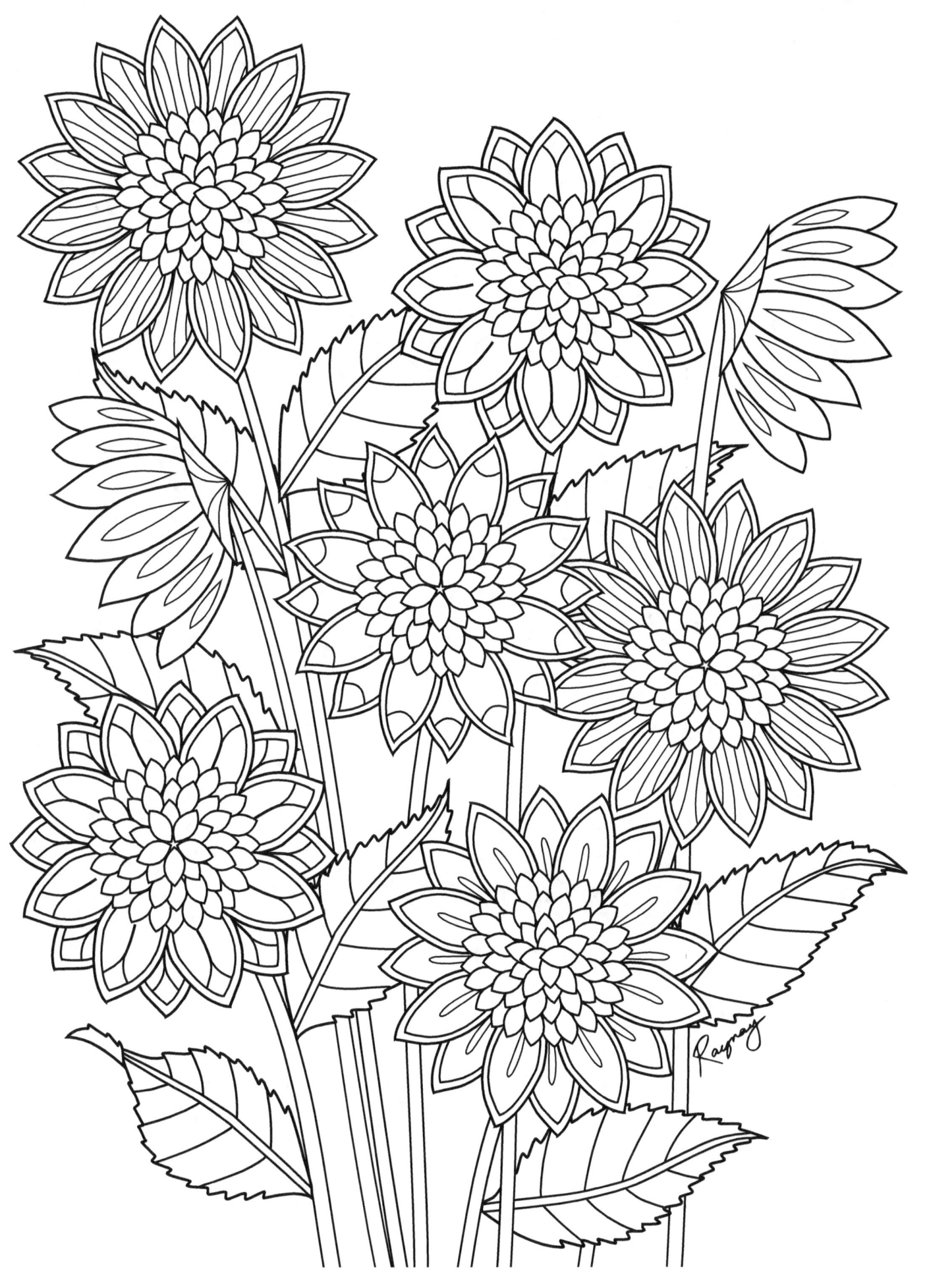

Title: The Willow and the Winding Path

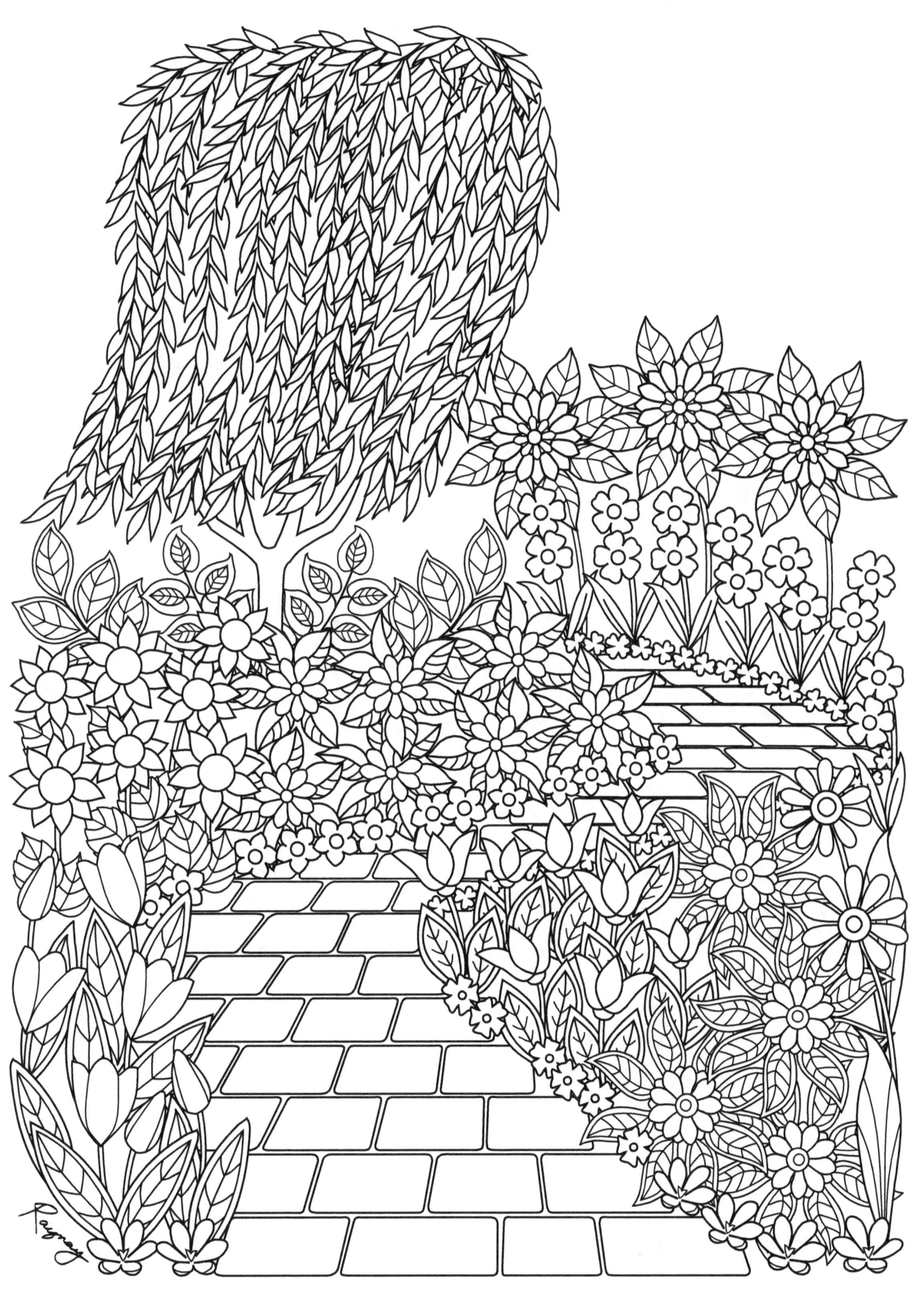

Title: Cat with a Butterfly

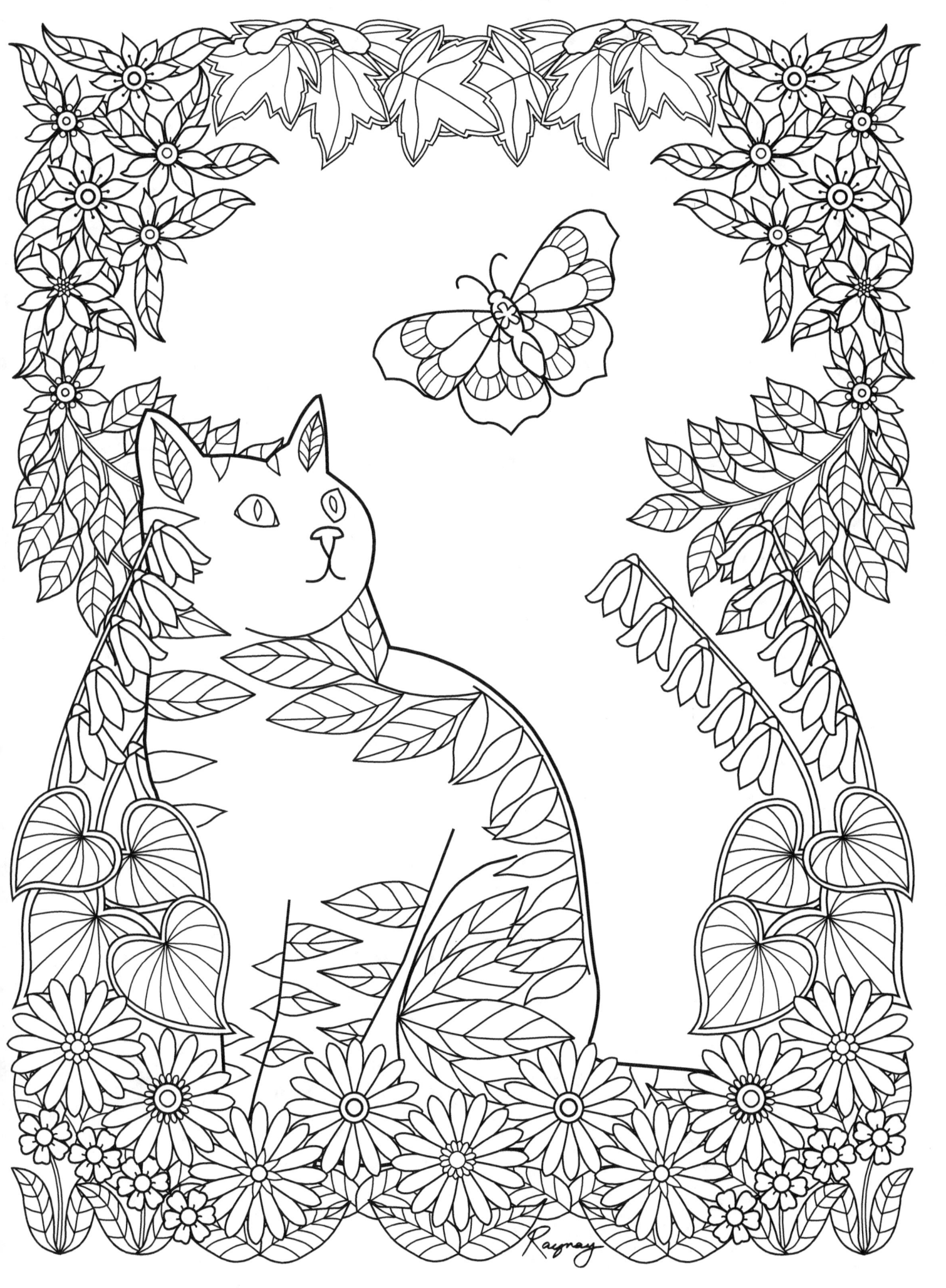

Title: Dove

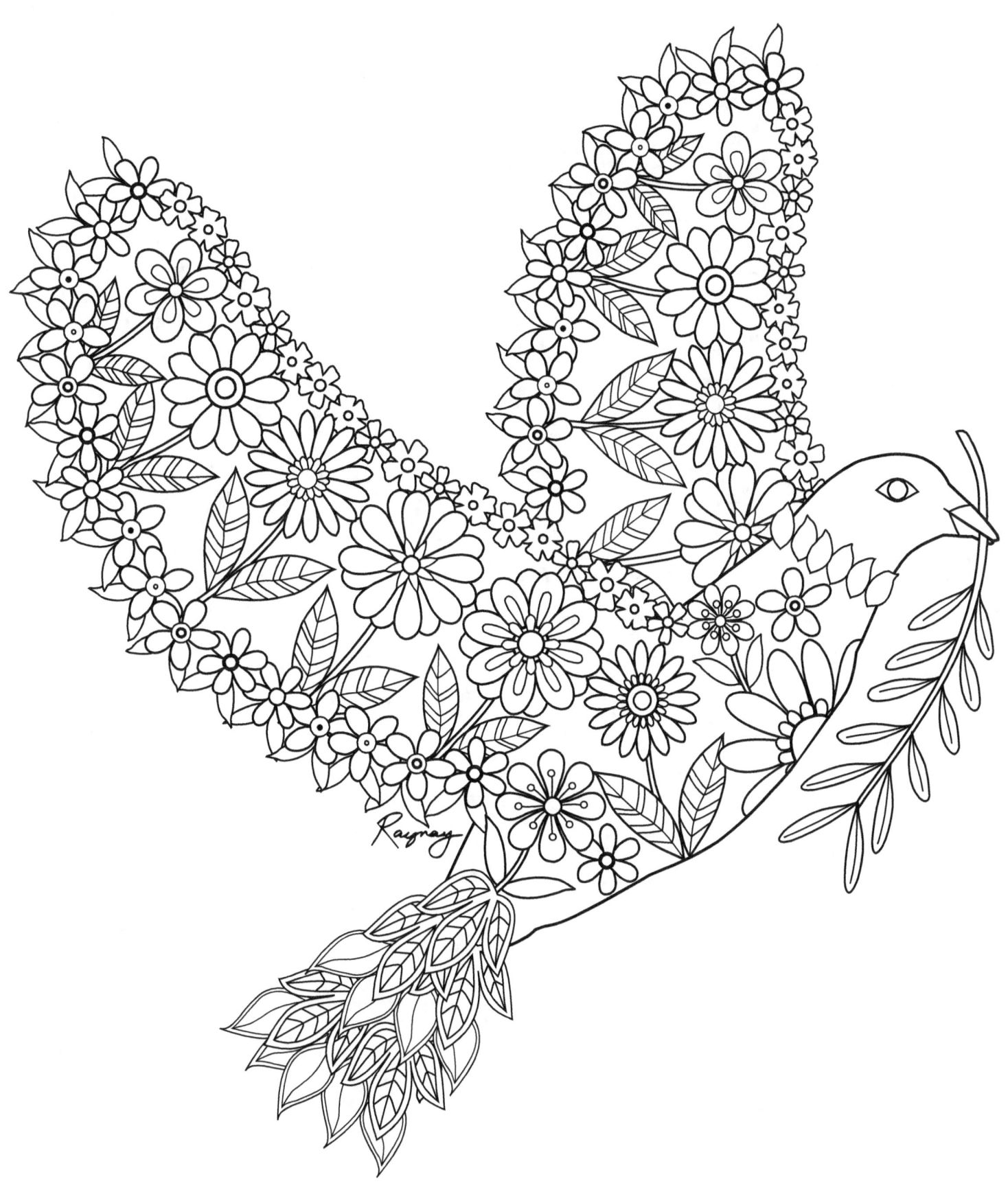

Title: The Birdhouse

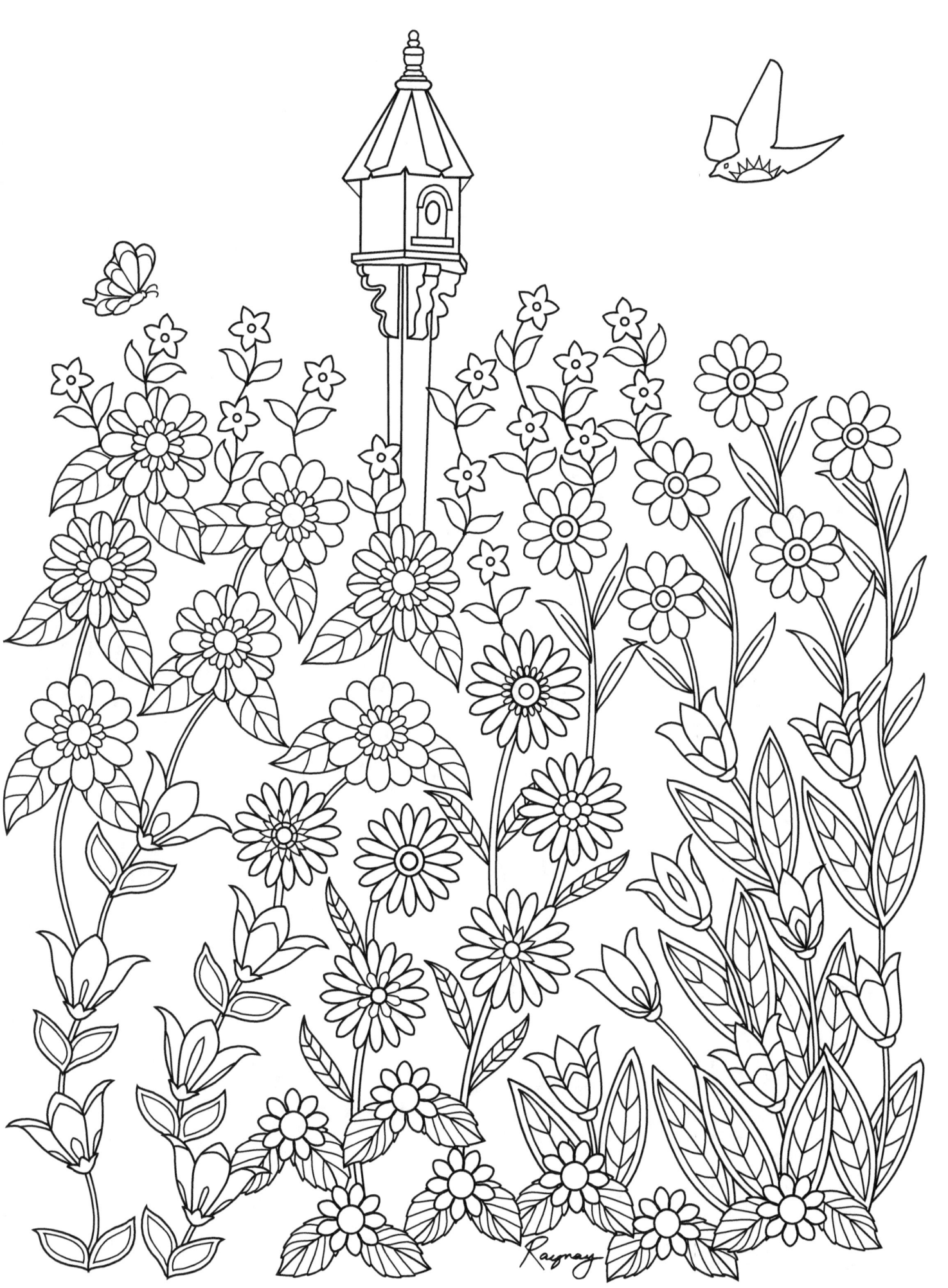

Title: Decorated Tree

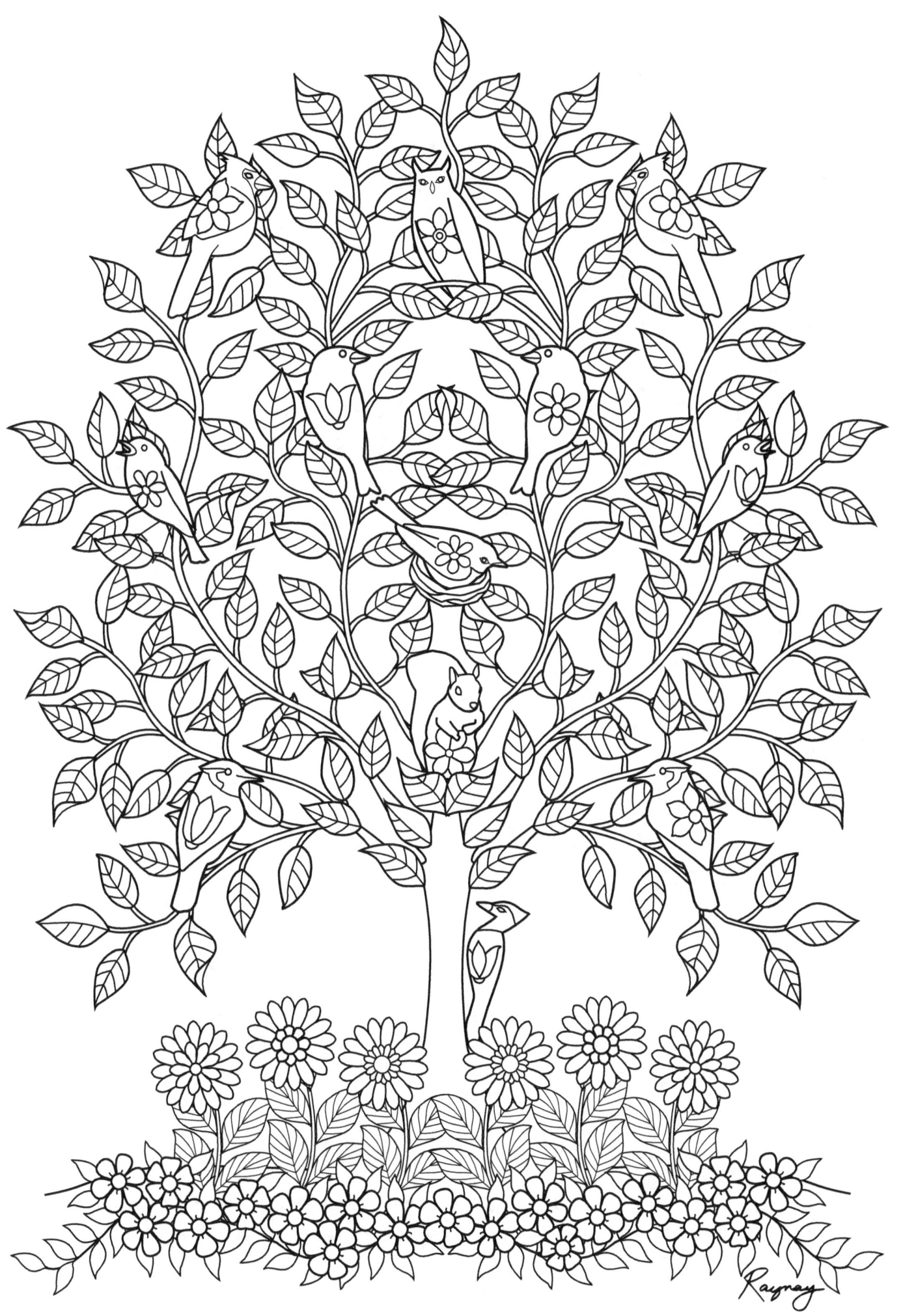

Title: Delightful Garden

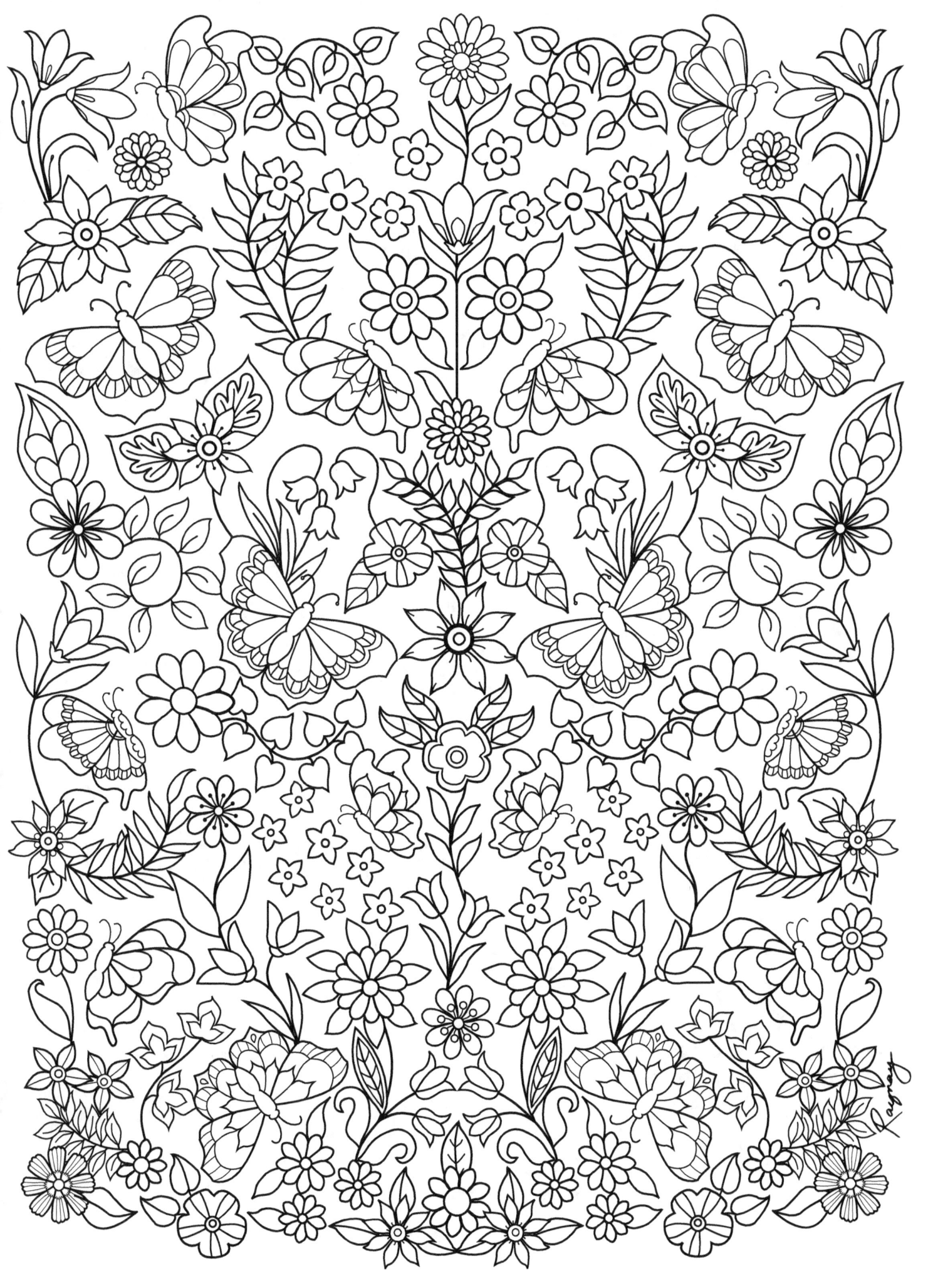

Title: Patchwork of Flowers

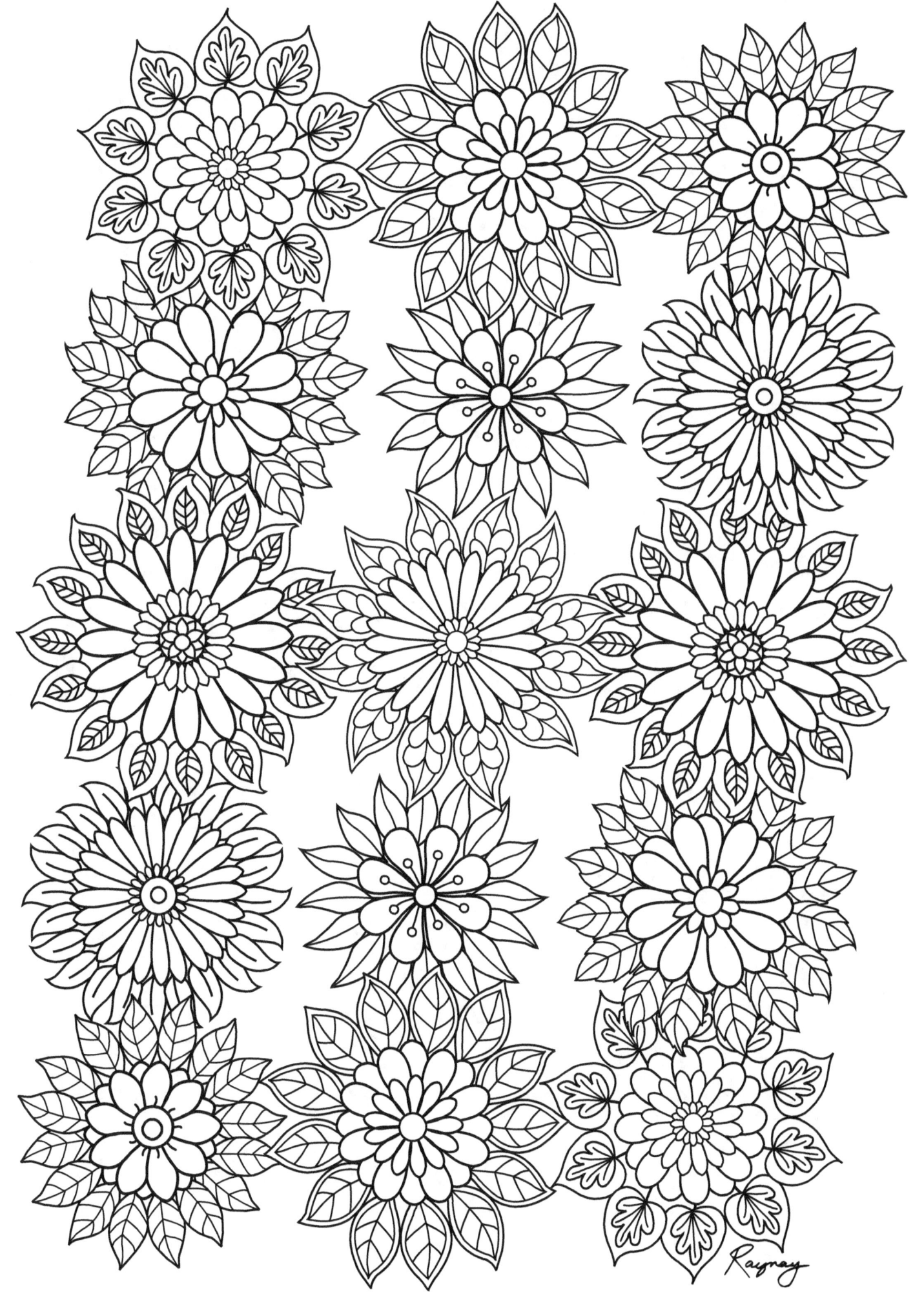

Title: Painted Elephant

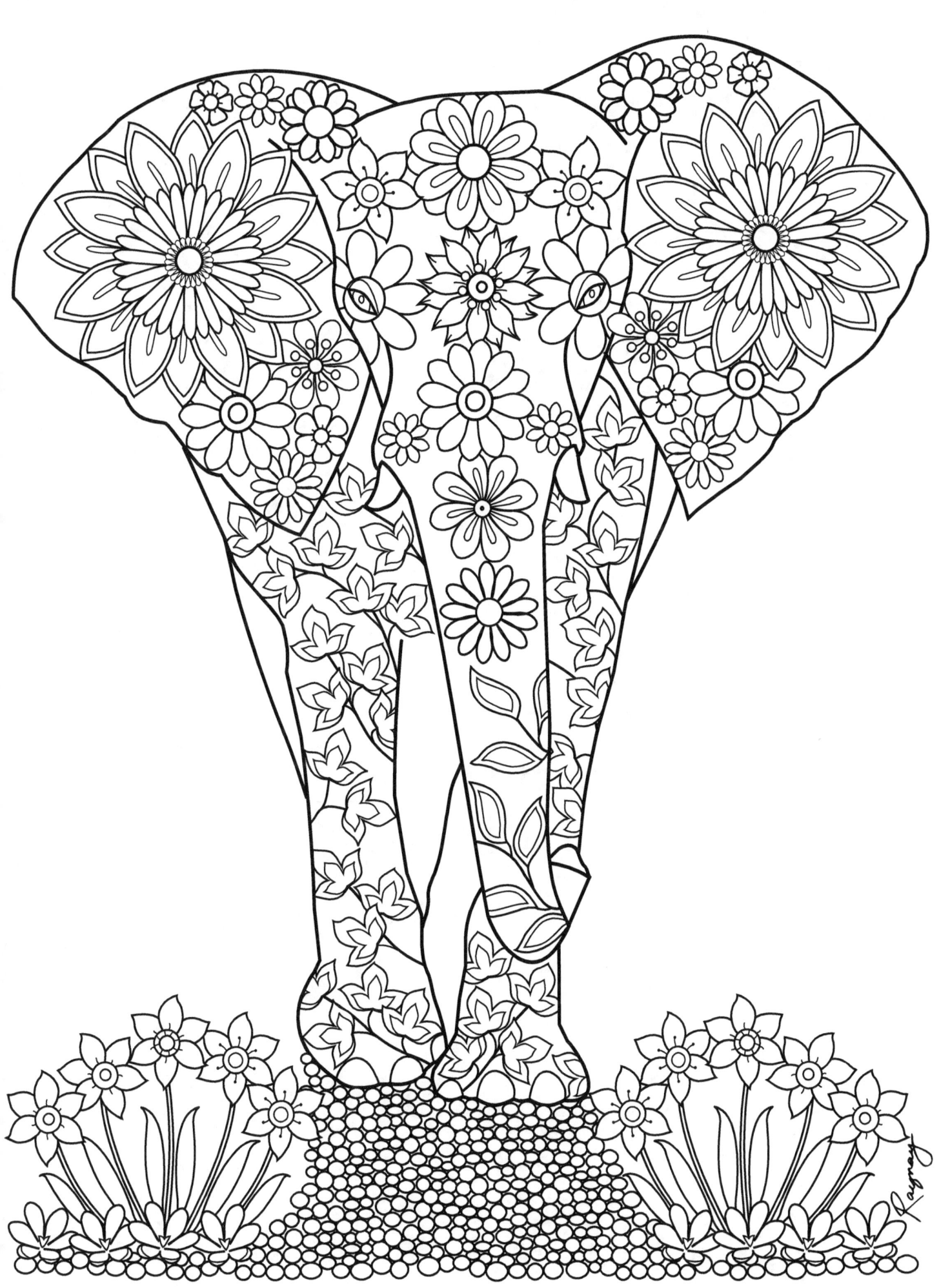

Title: Yorkie

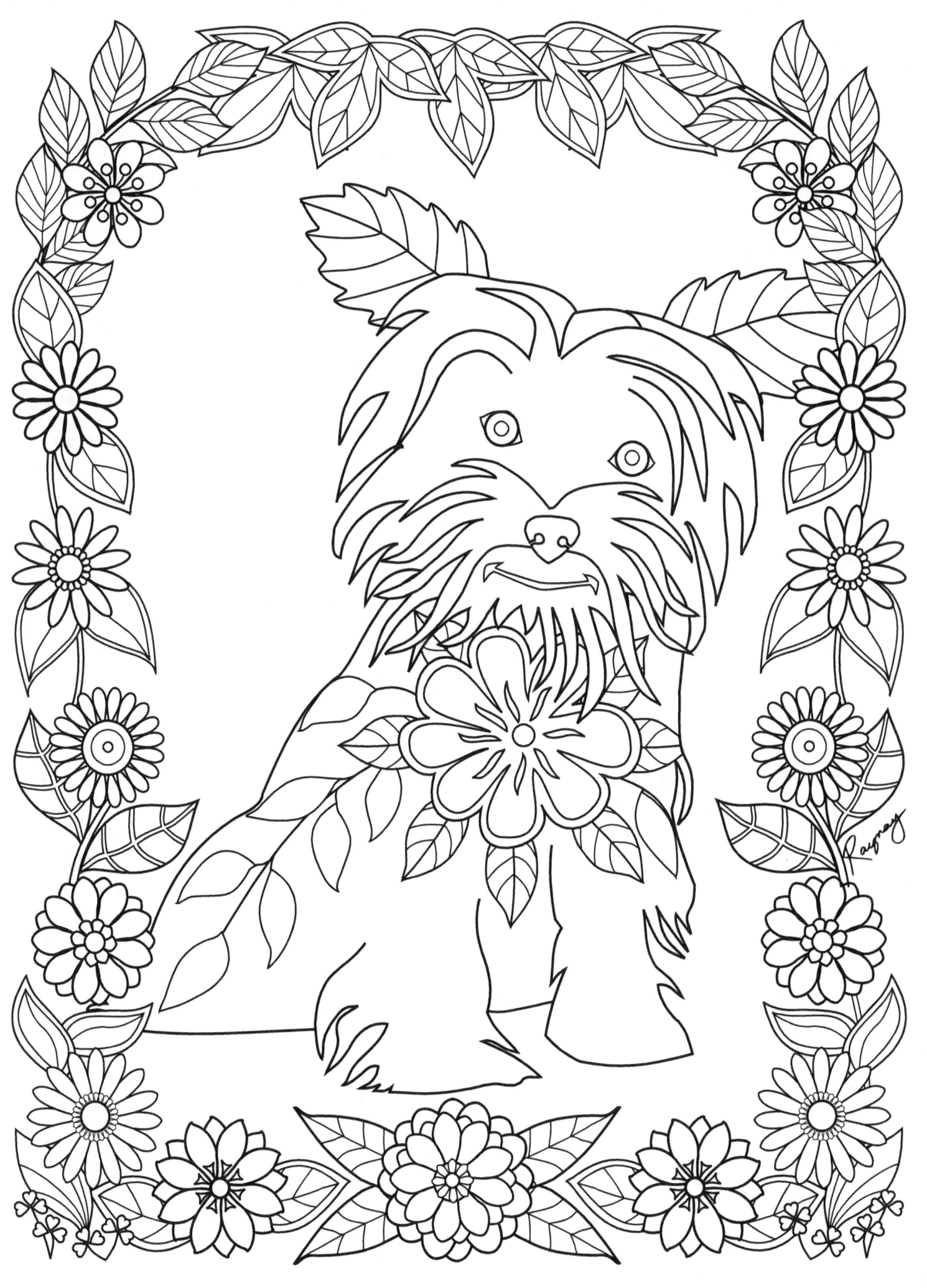

Title: Container Gardens

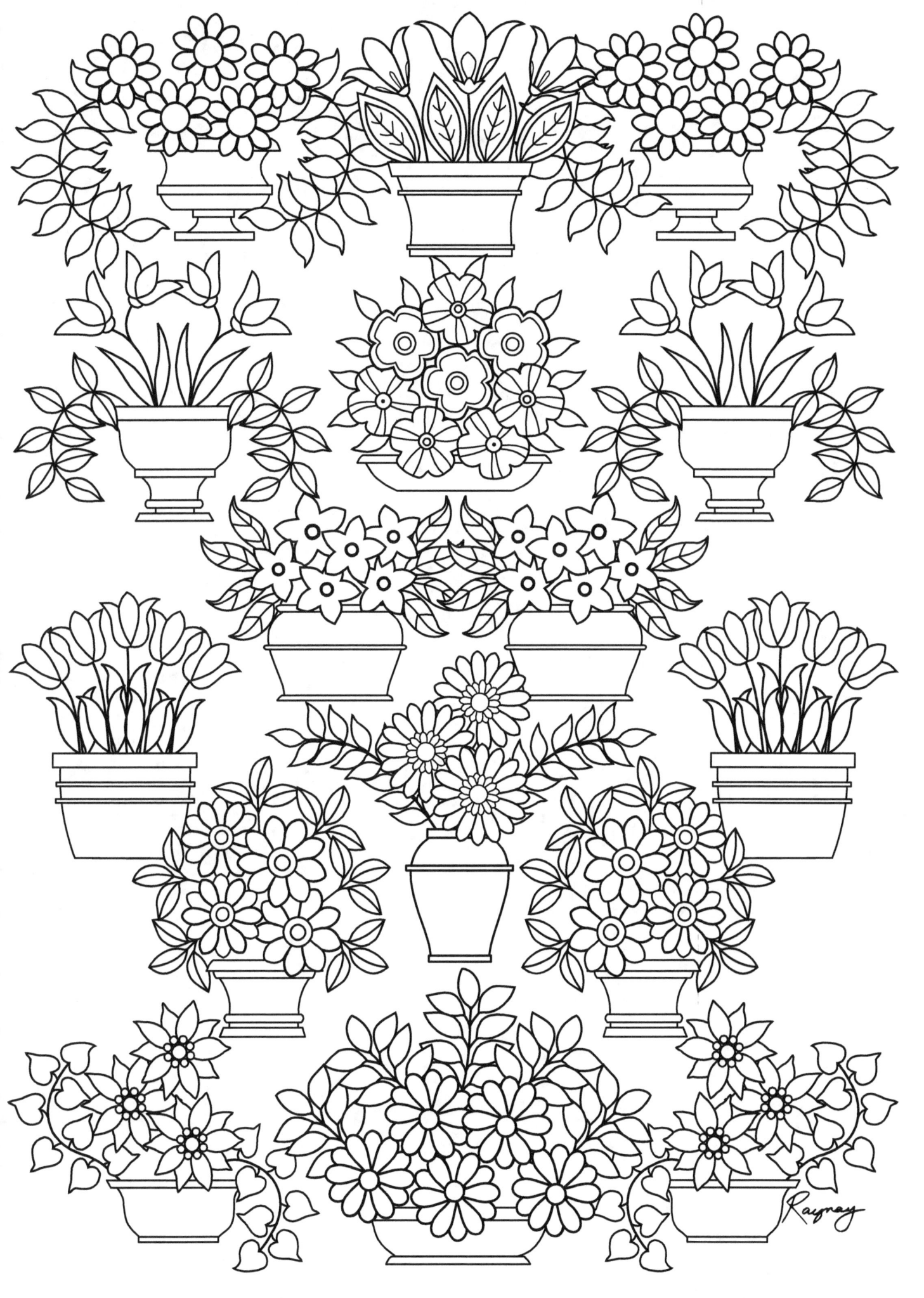

Title: Butterflies Welcome

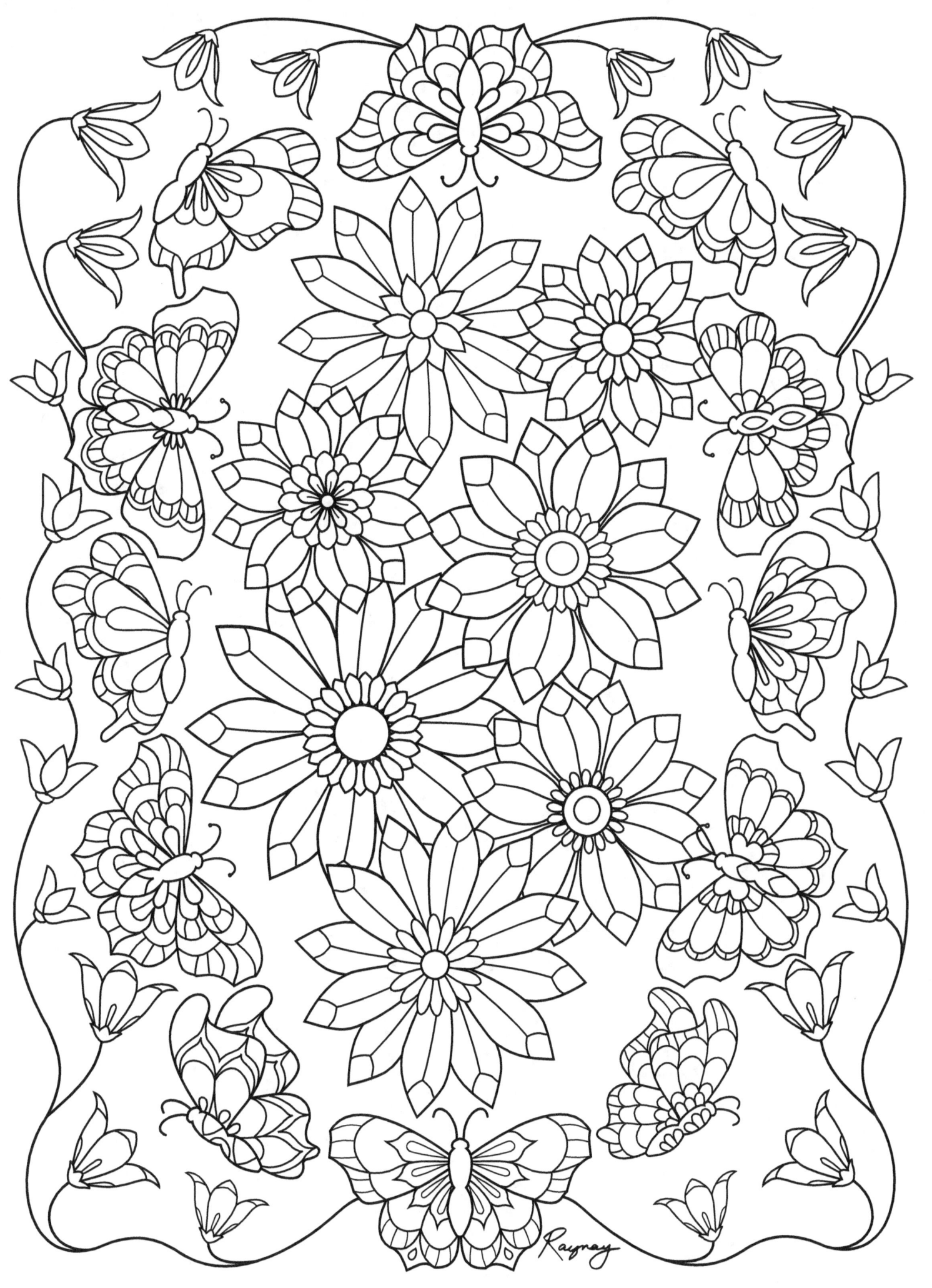

Title: Leafy Star

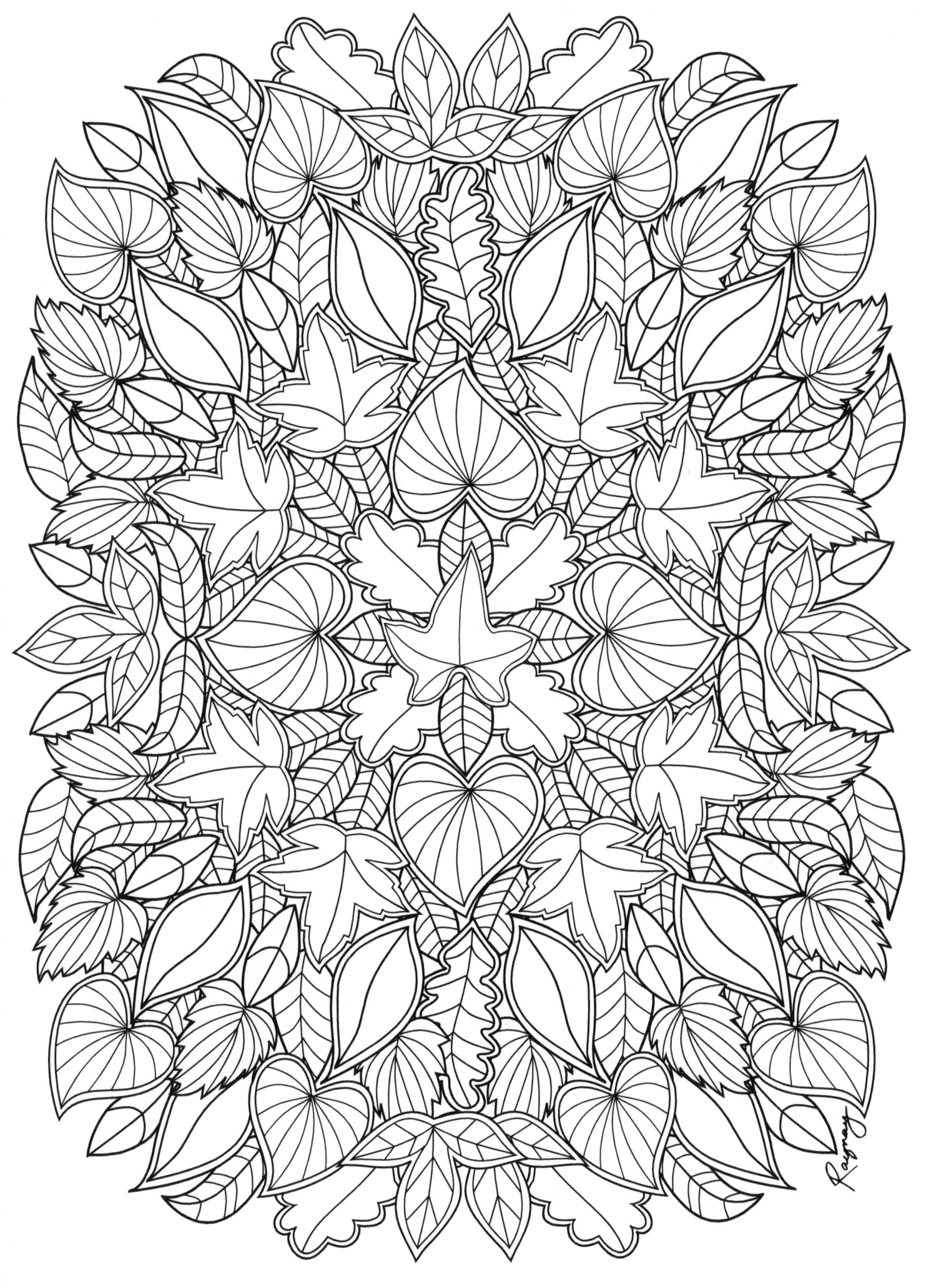

Title: Wolf and Moon

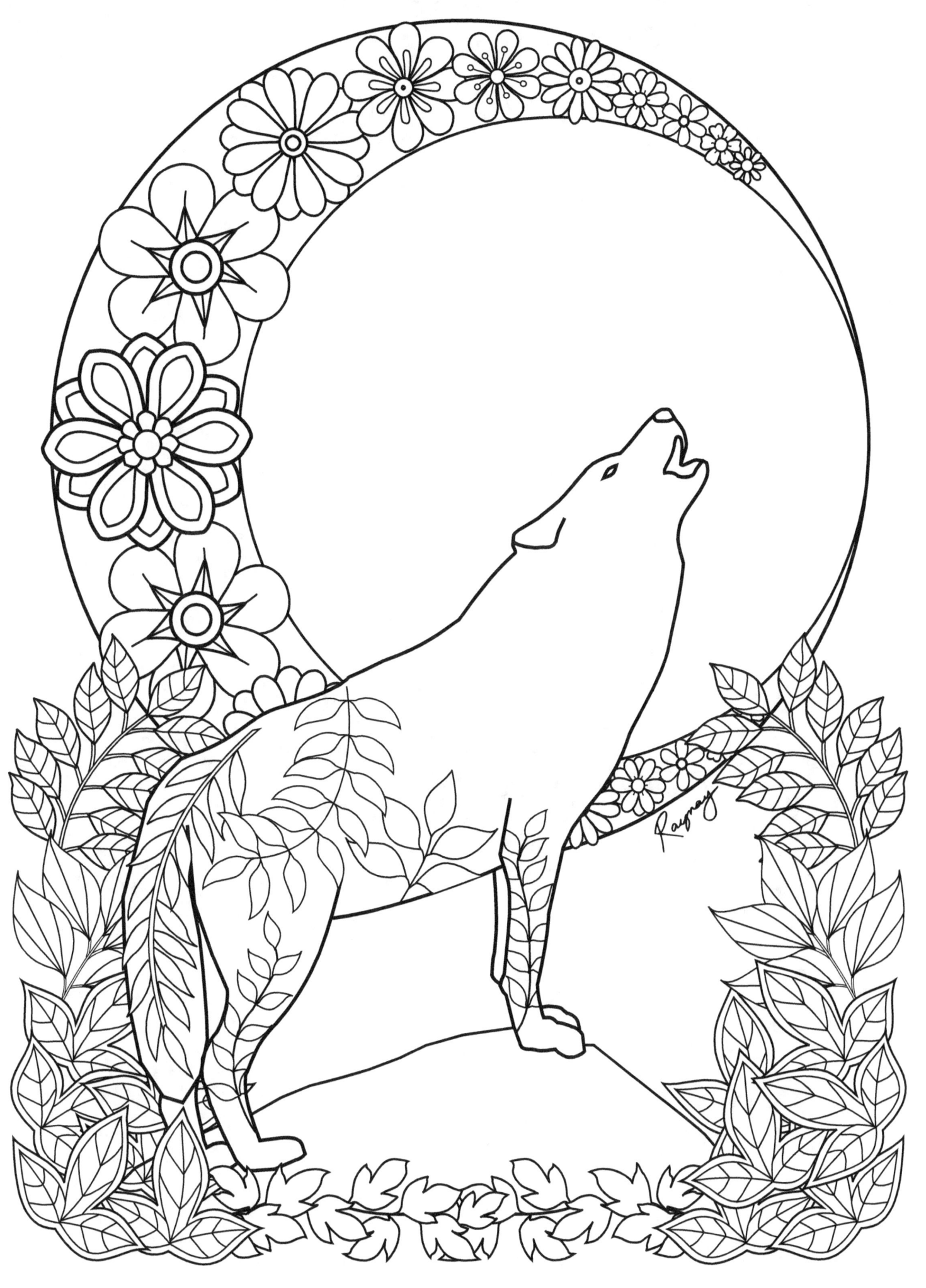

Title: Flower Patches

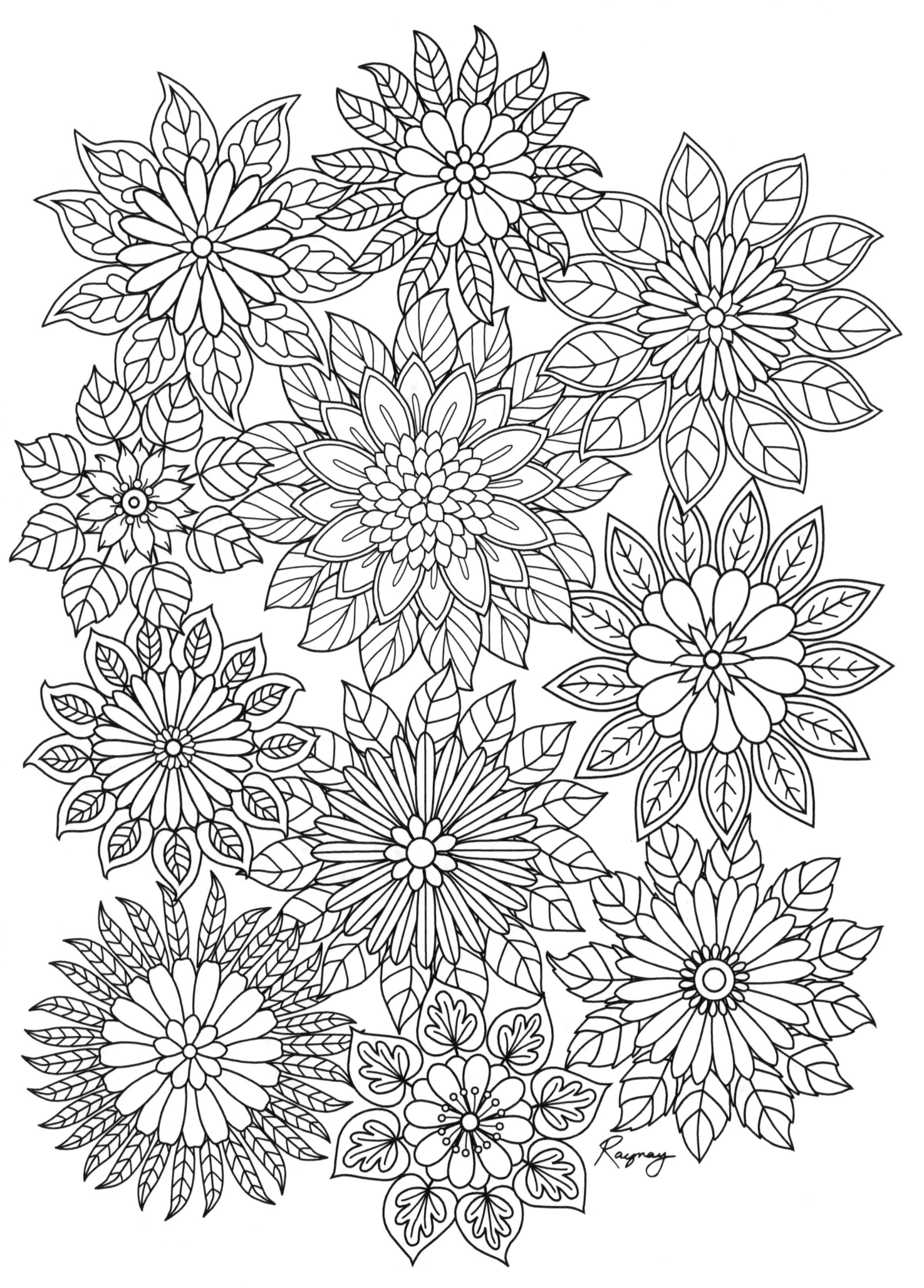

Title: Spring Tree

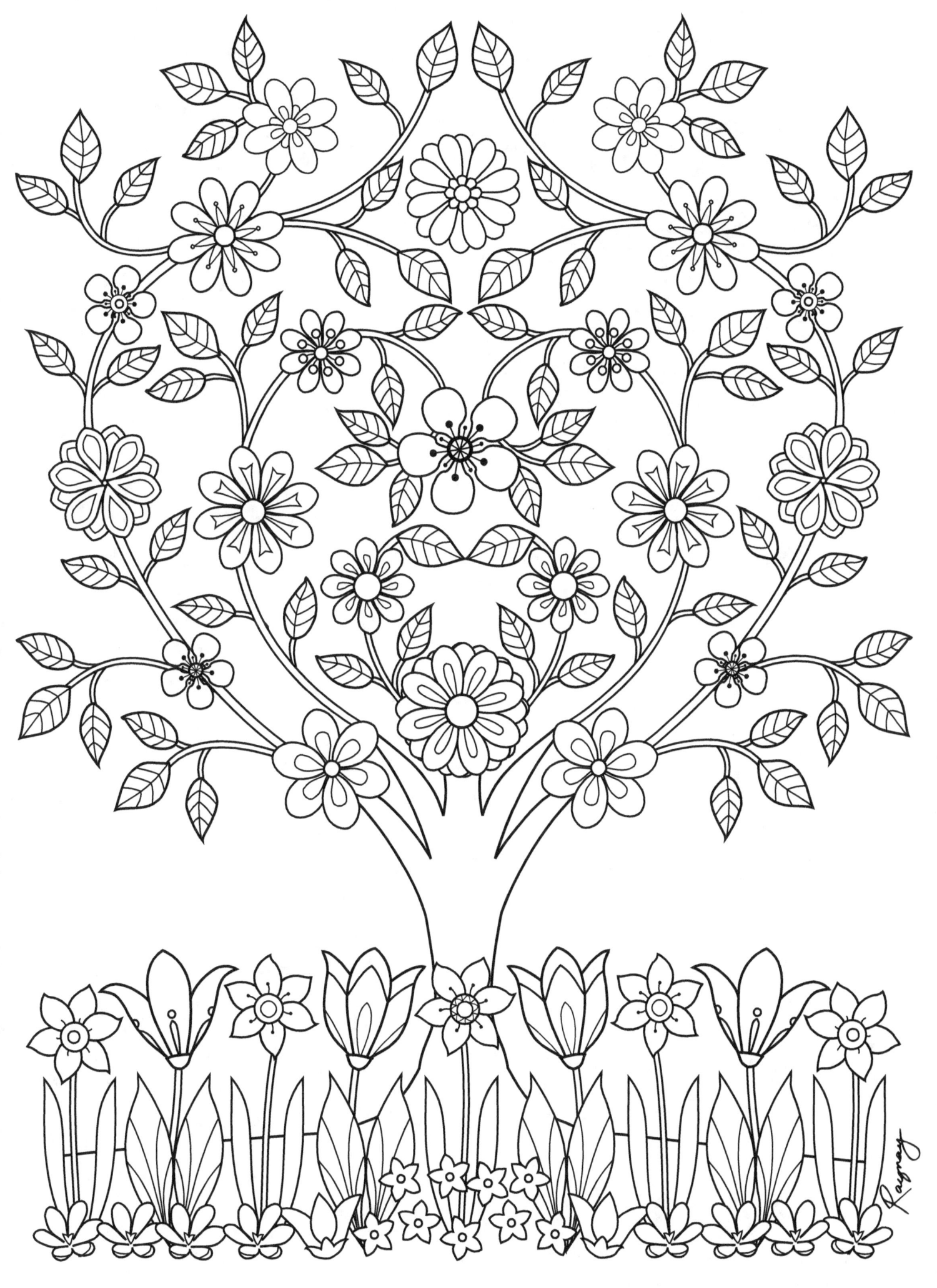

Title: Flower Bouquet

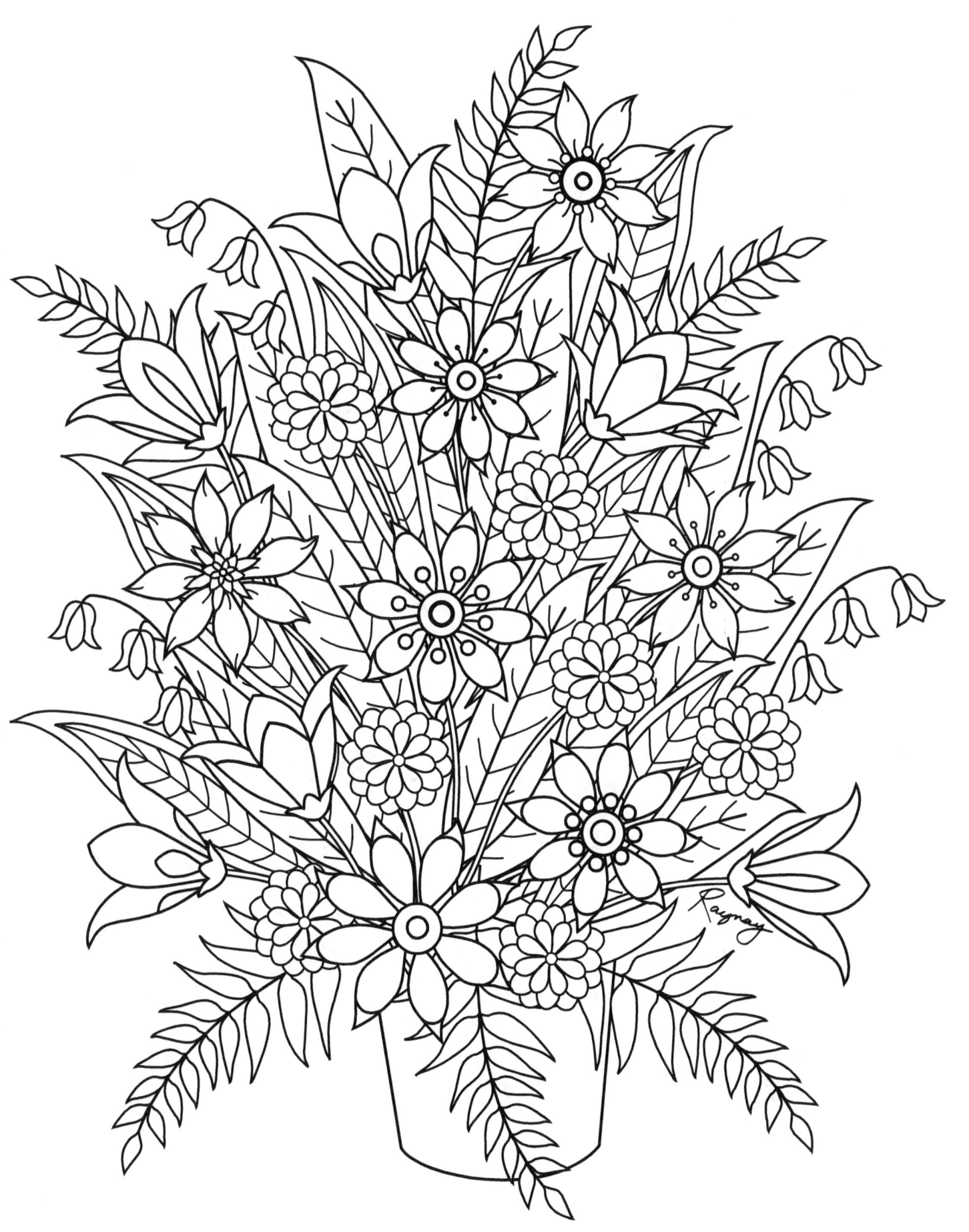

Title: The Birdbath

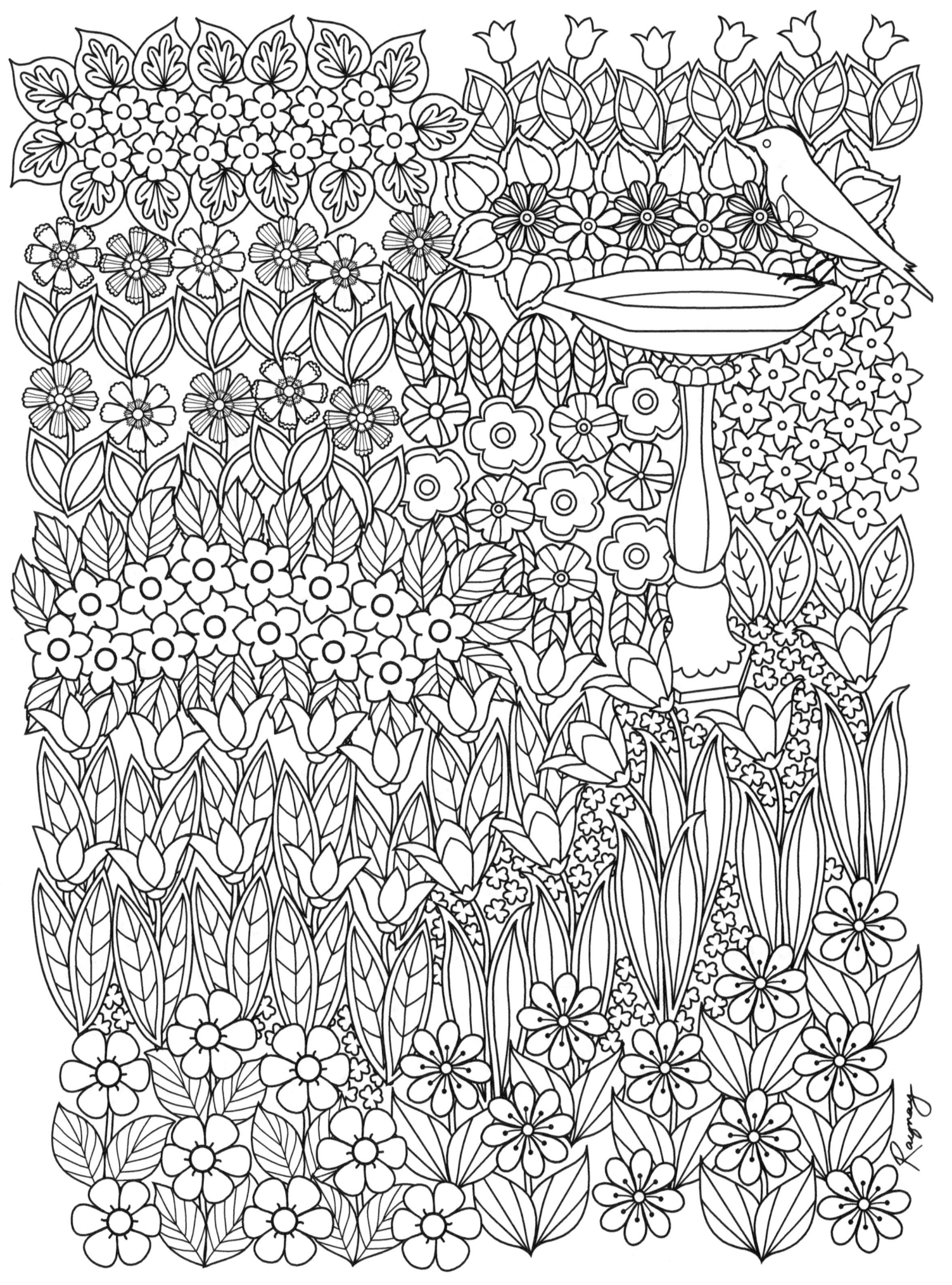

Title: The Little Lamb

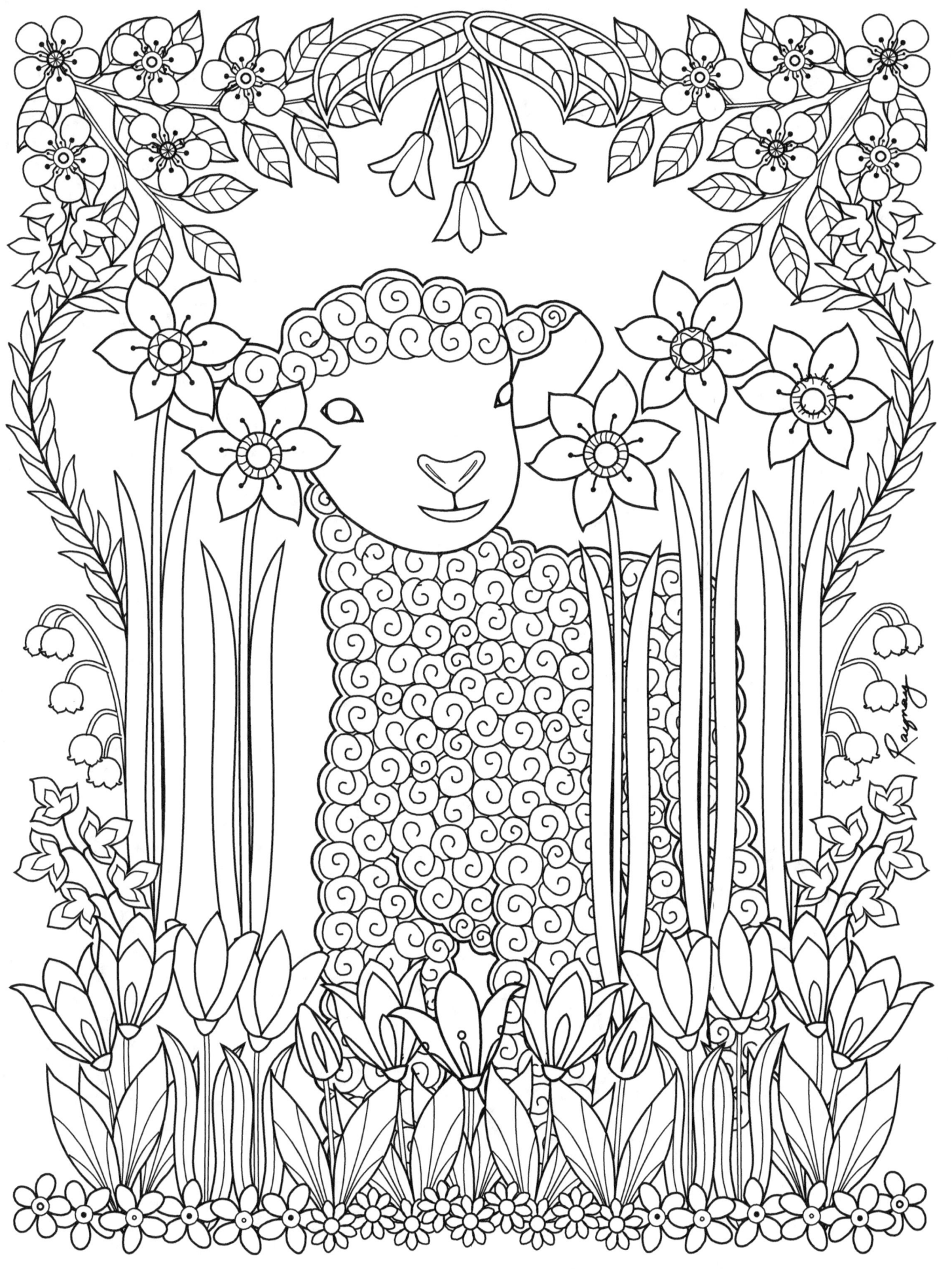

Title: The Vases

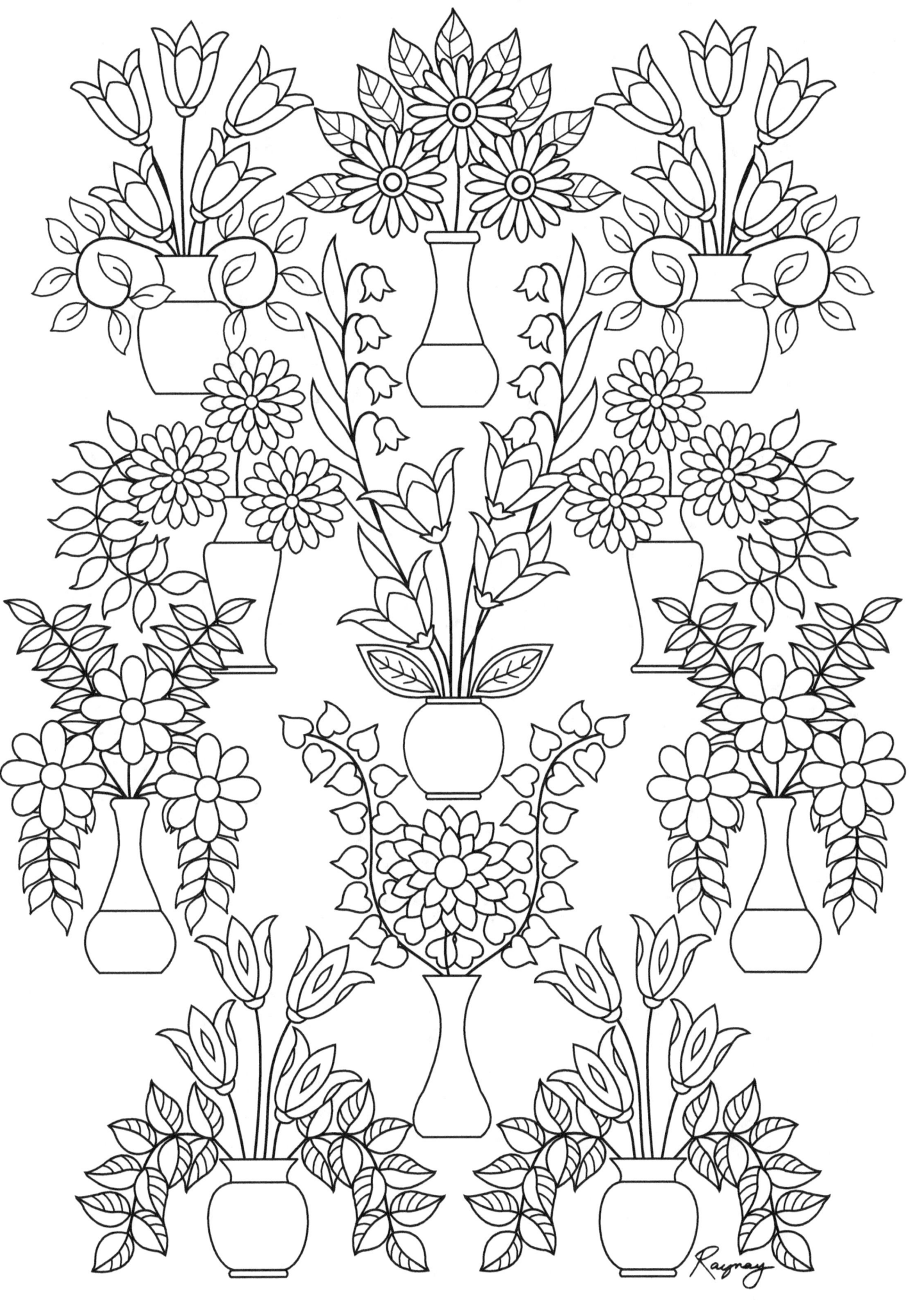

Title: Run of the Garden

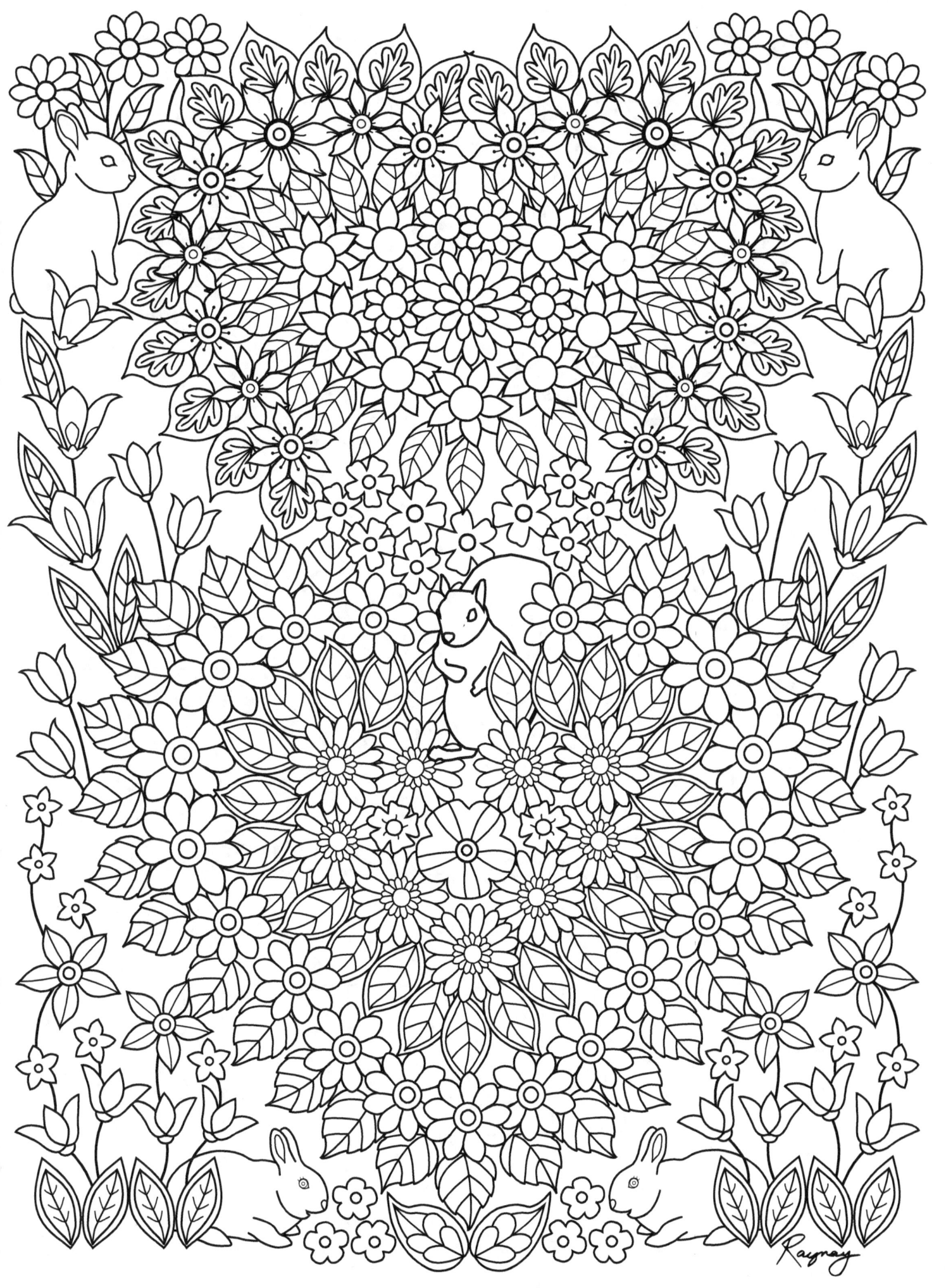

Title: Star Flower

Title: The Dragonfly

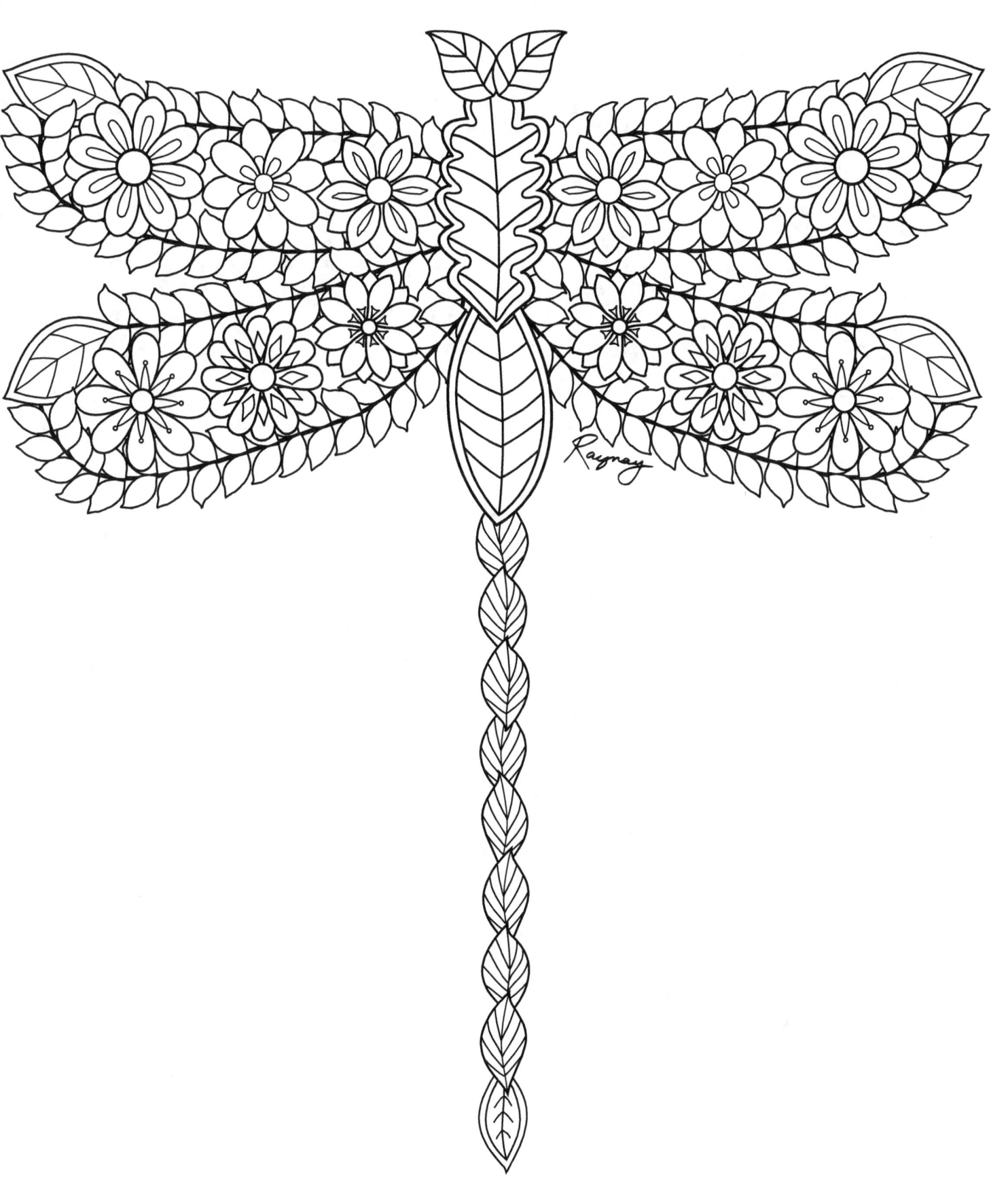

Title: Vine of Blooms

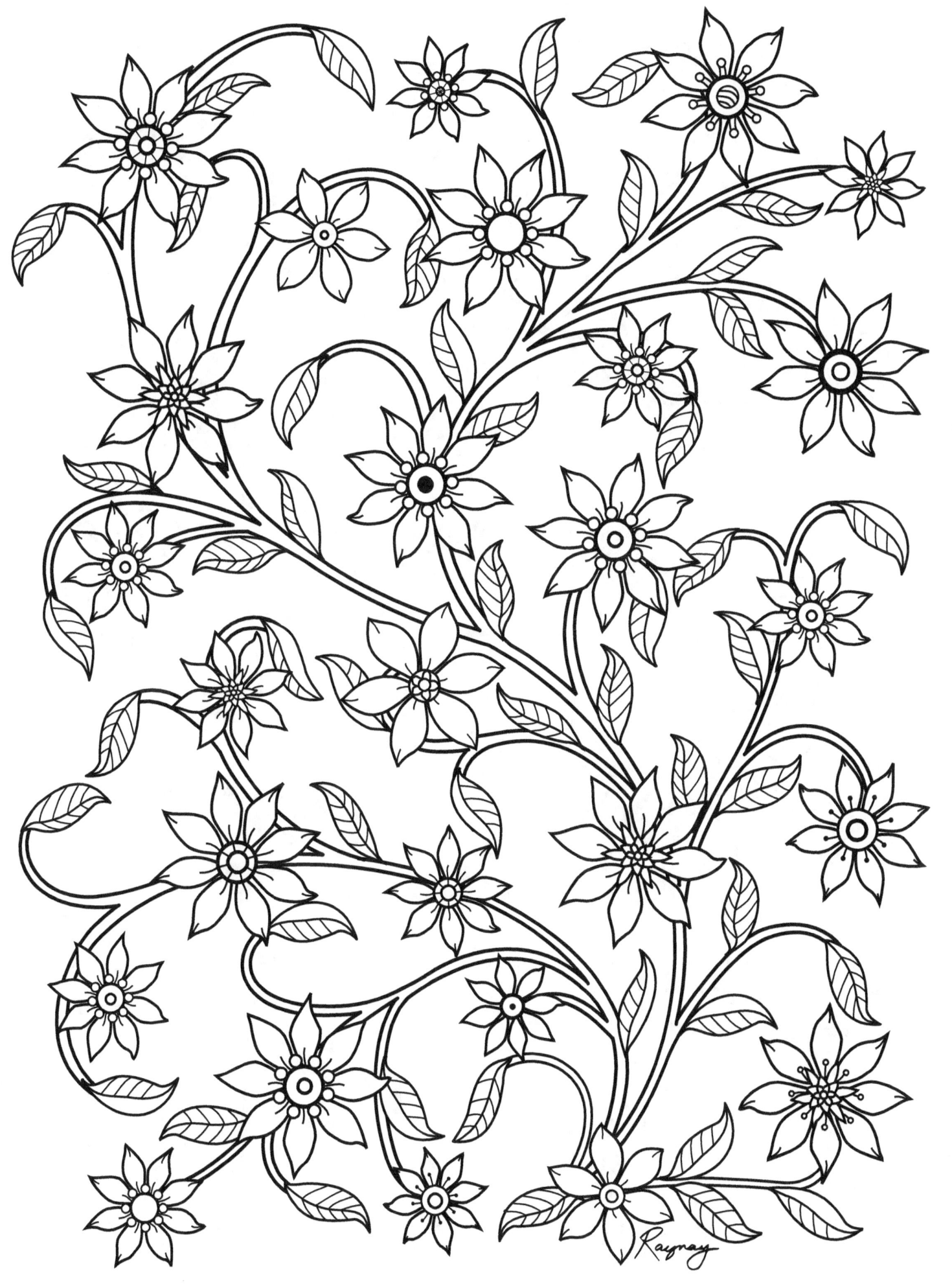

Title: Wildflower Patch

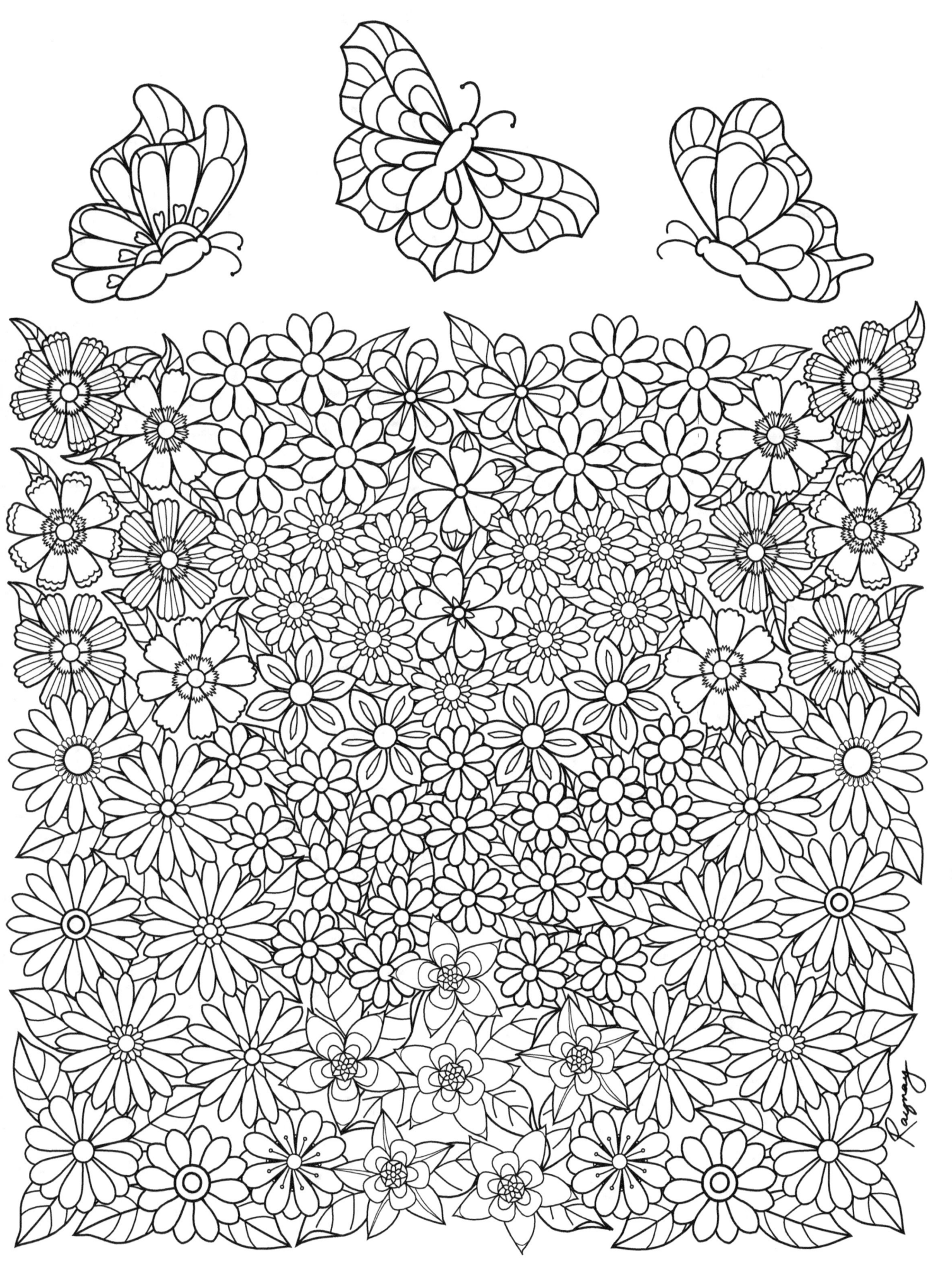

Title: The Bird's Nest

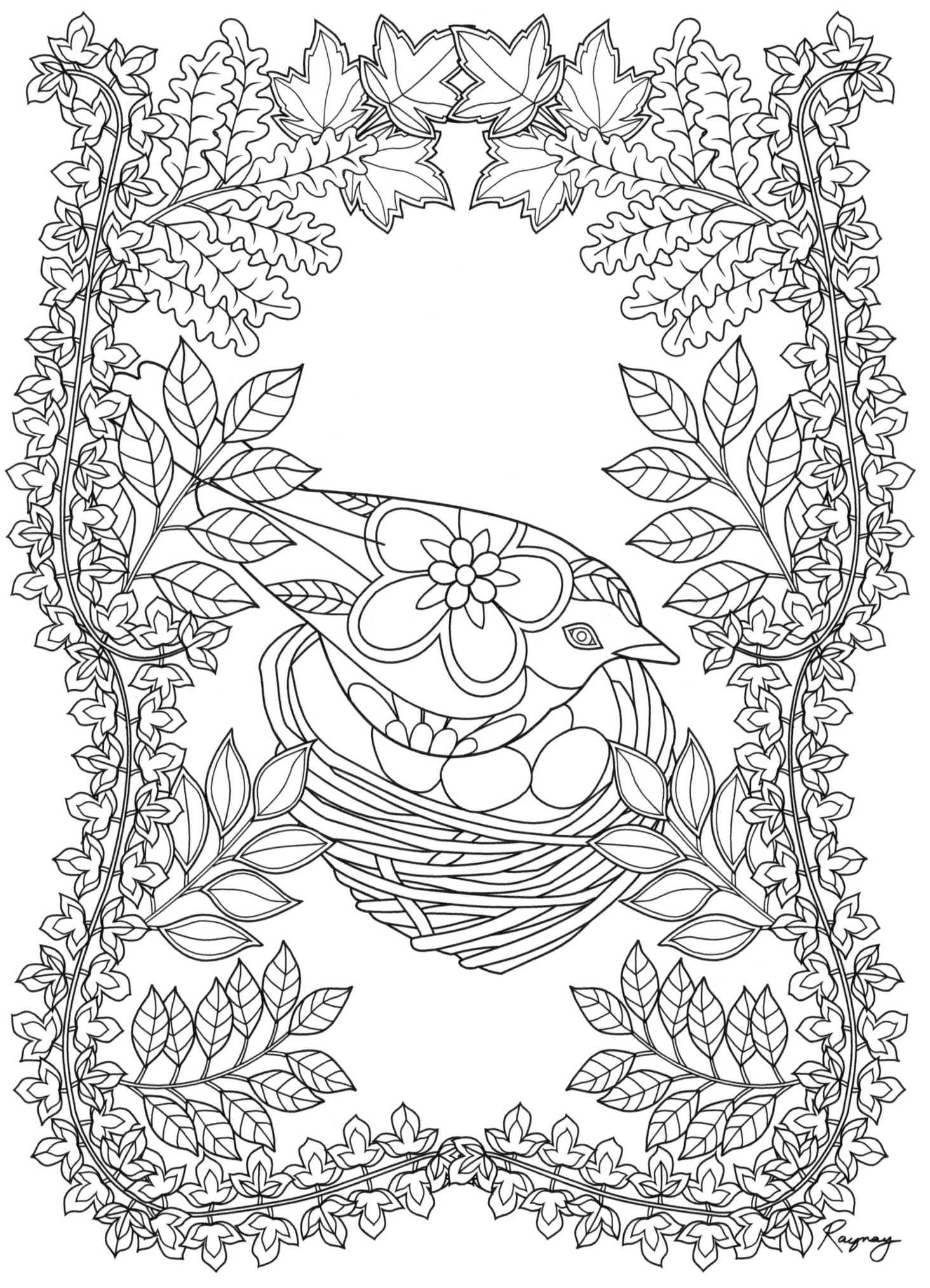

Title: Big Flower Patch

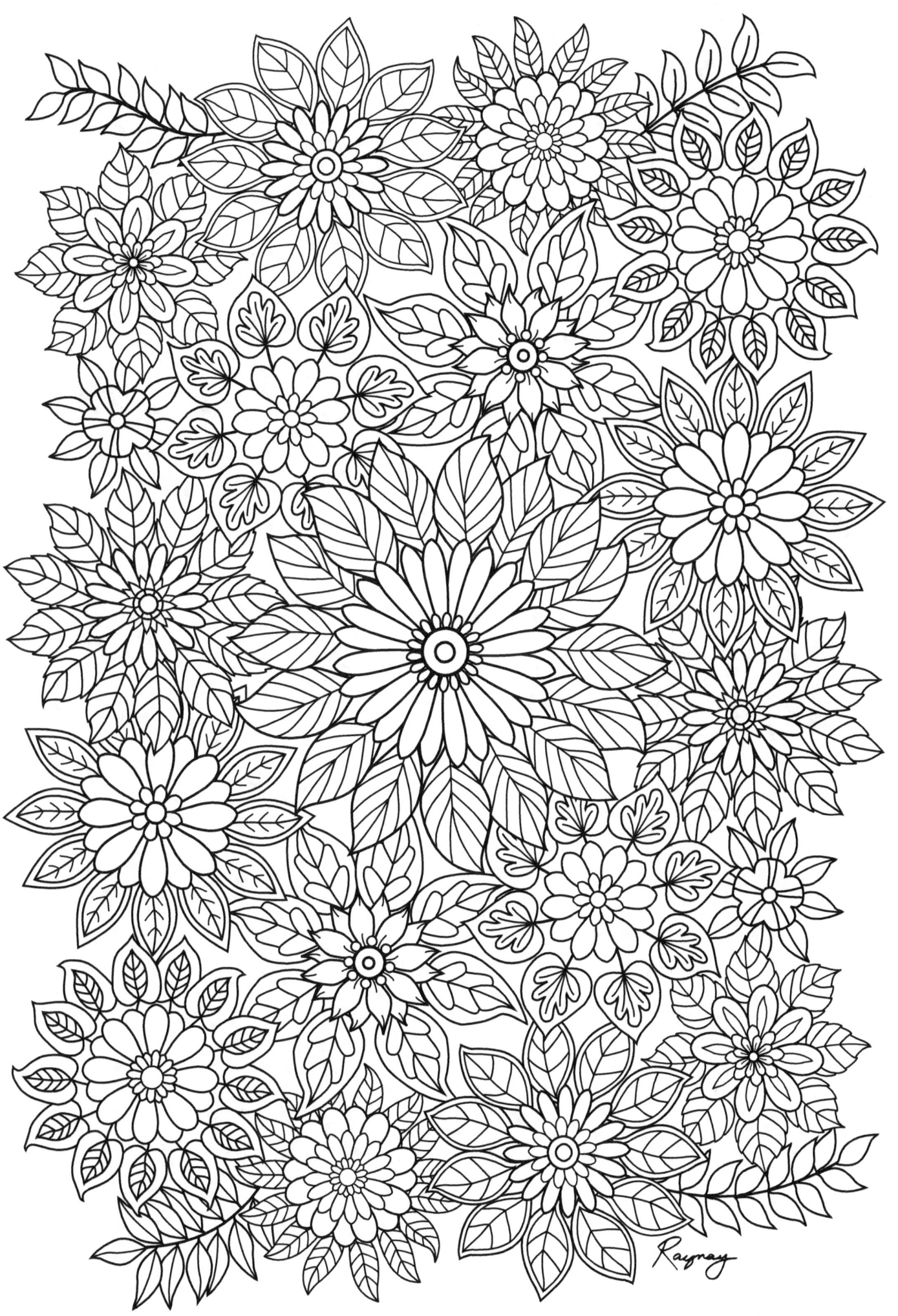

Title: Butterfly Dance

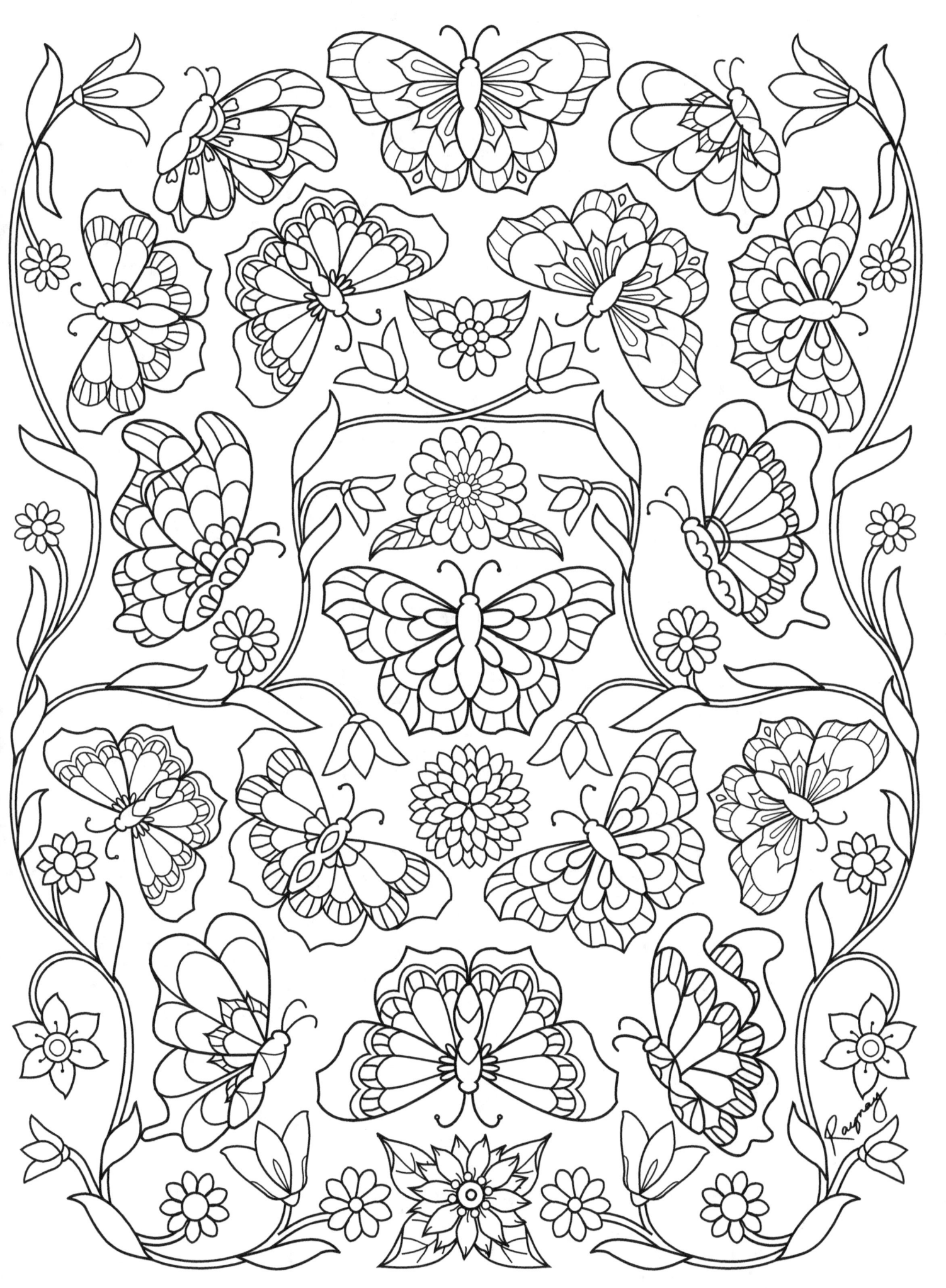

Title: The Horses

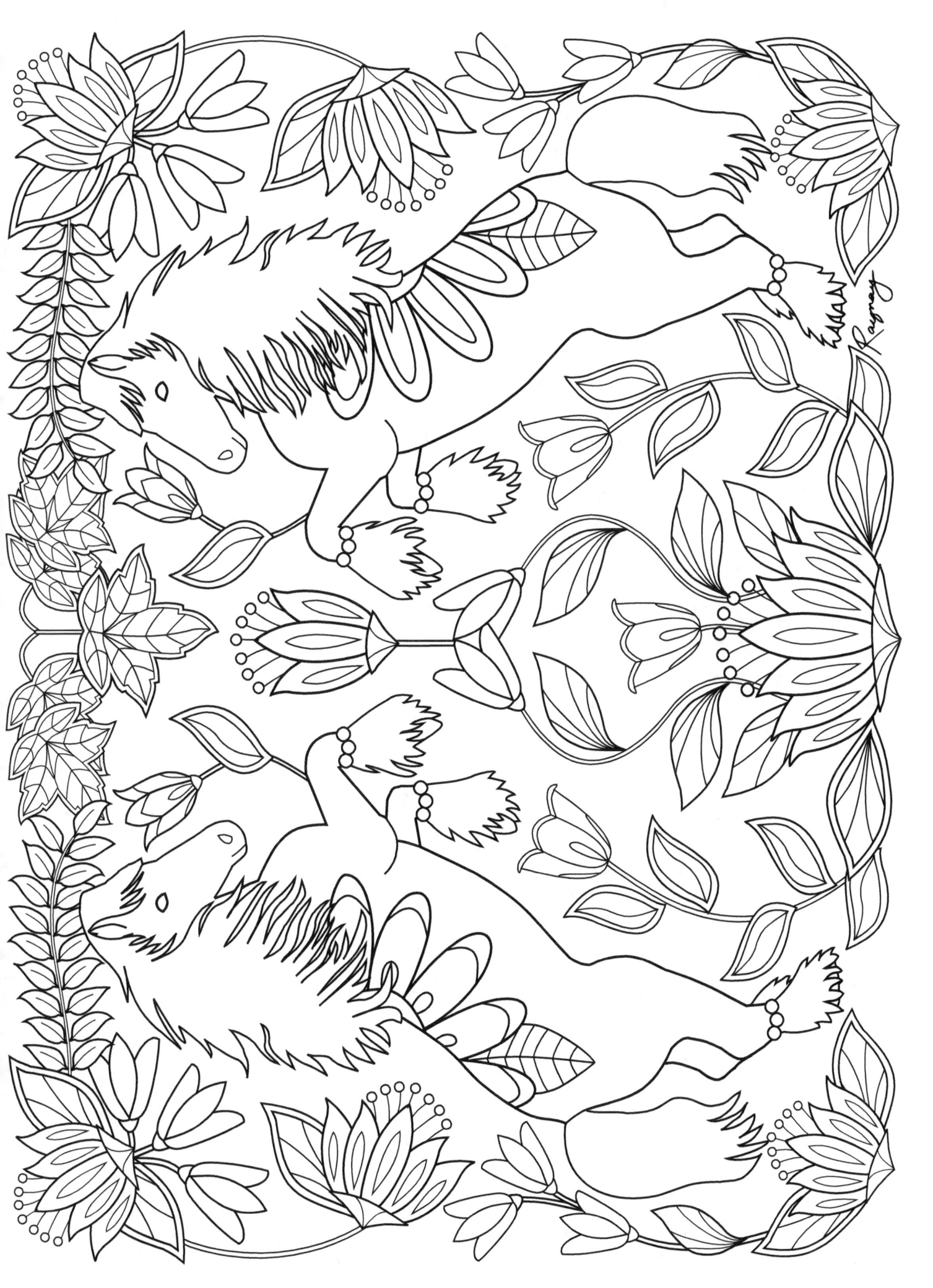

Title: The Stray in the Groundcover

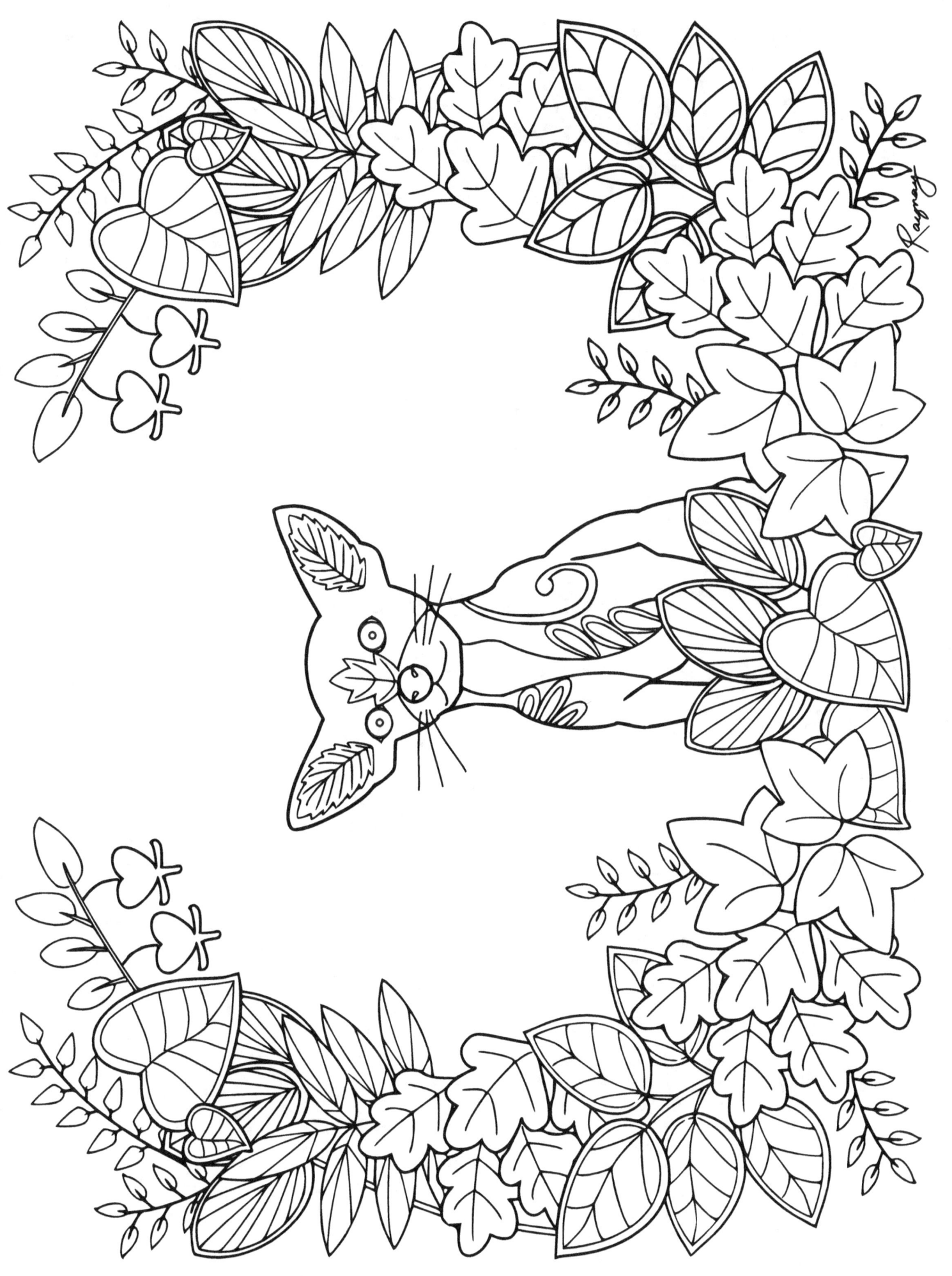

Title: Being in Love

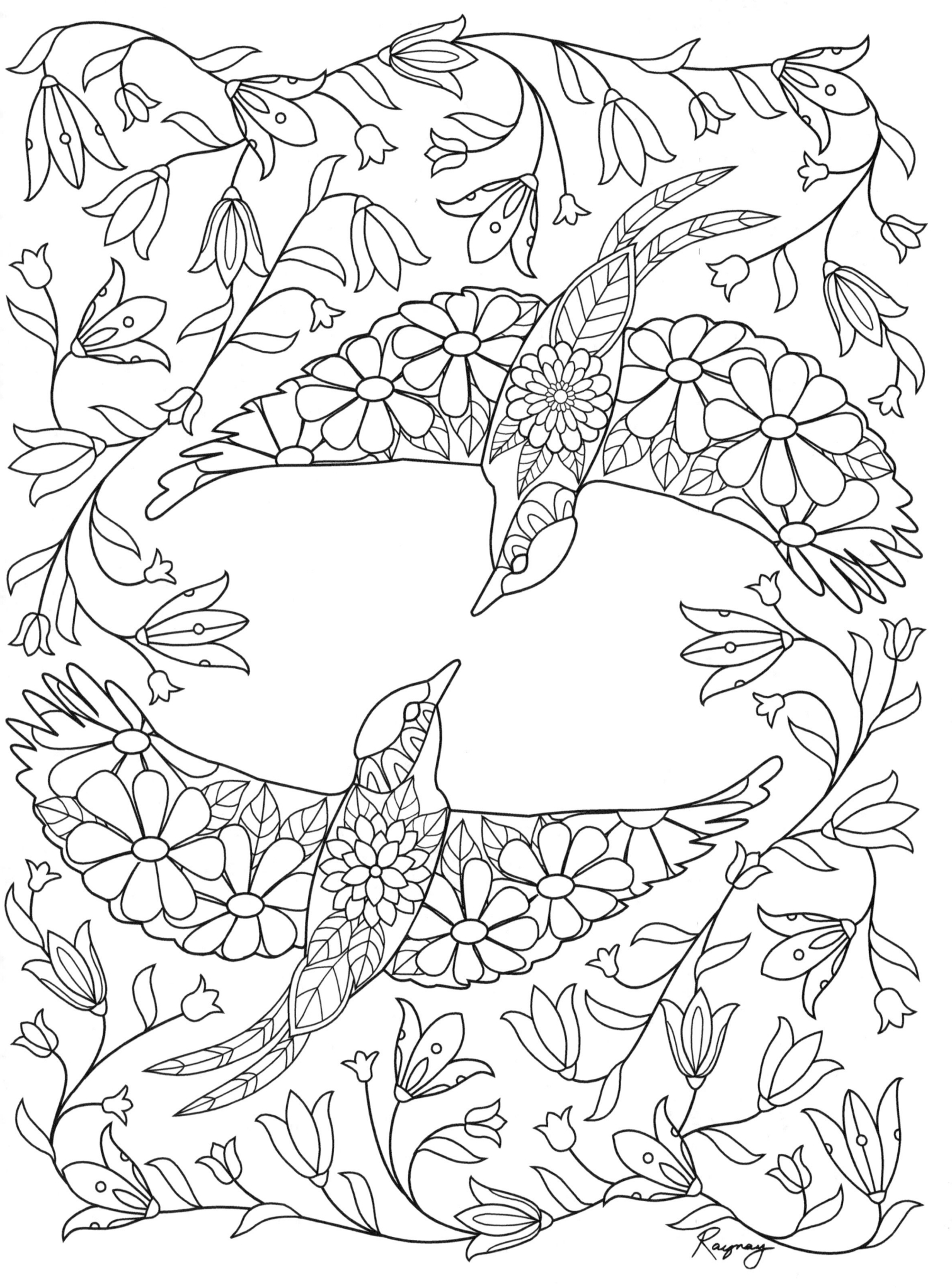

Title: Squirrels

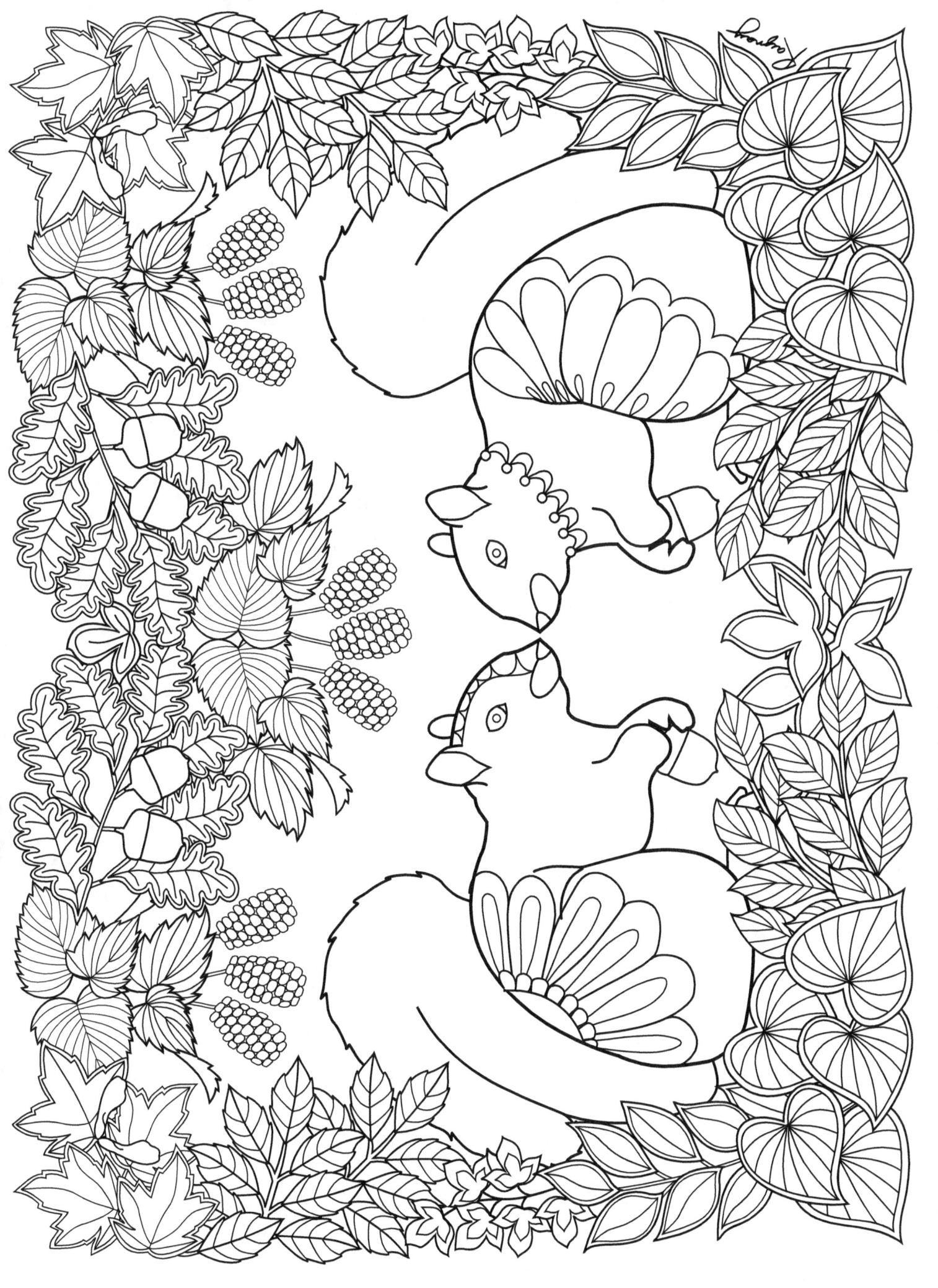

Title: The Garden Steps

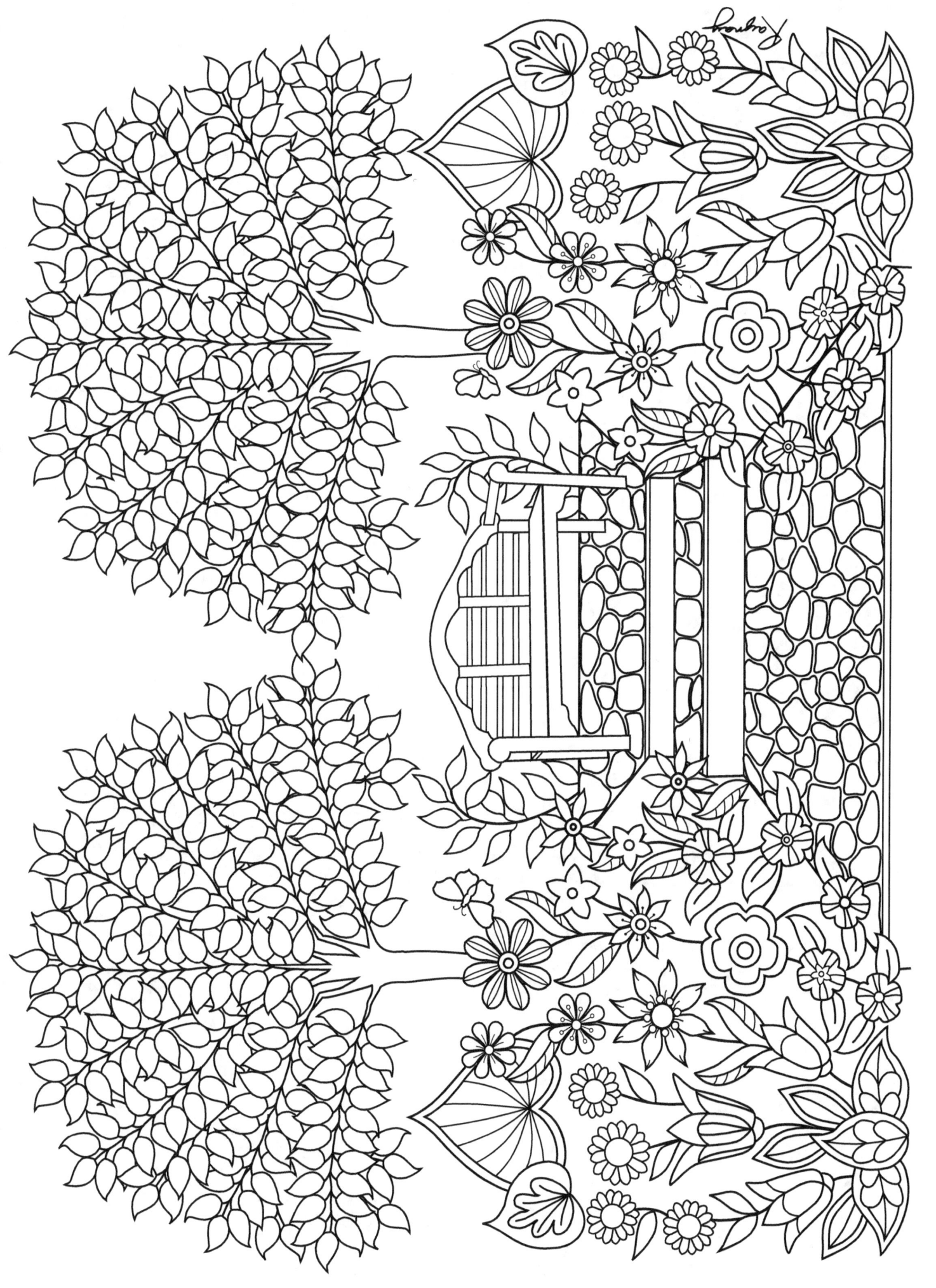

Title: Flower Line

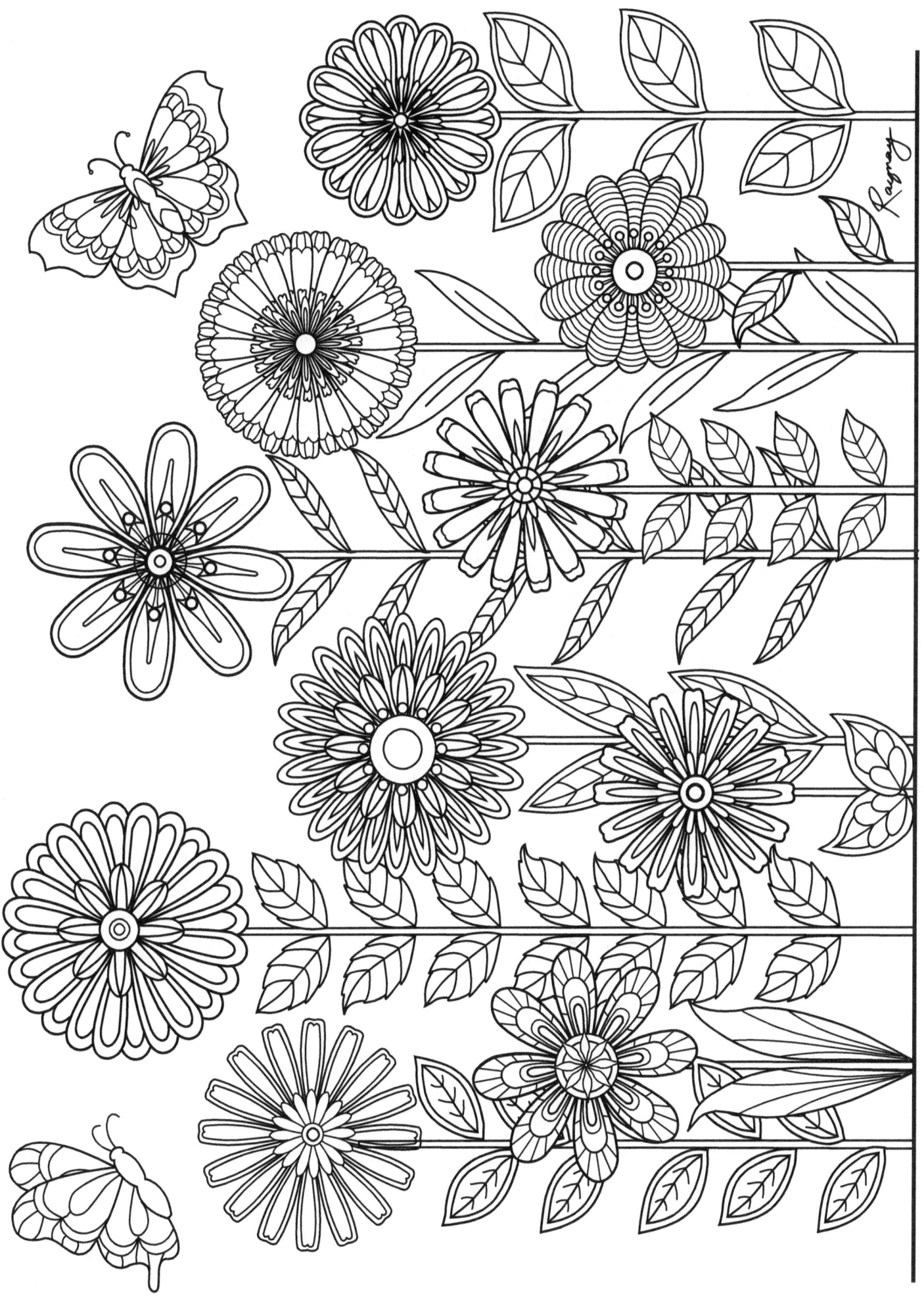

Title: The Rabbits

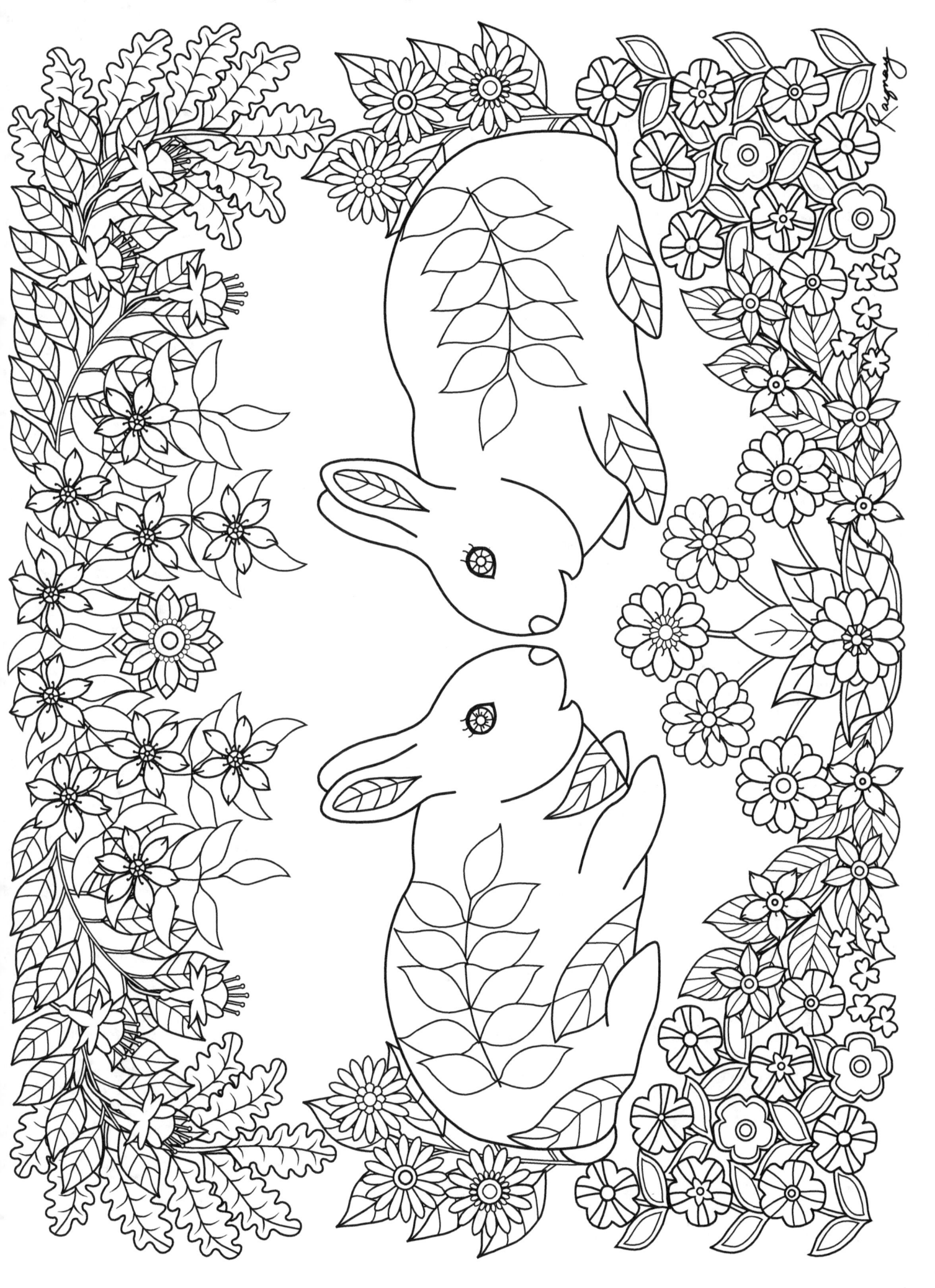

Title: Parrot Soaring

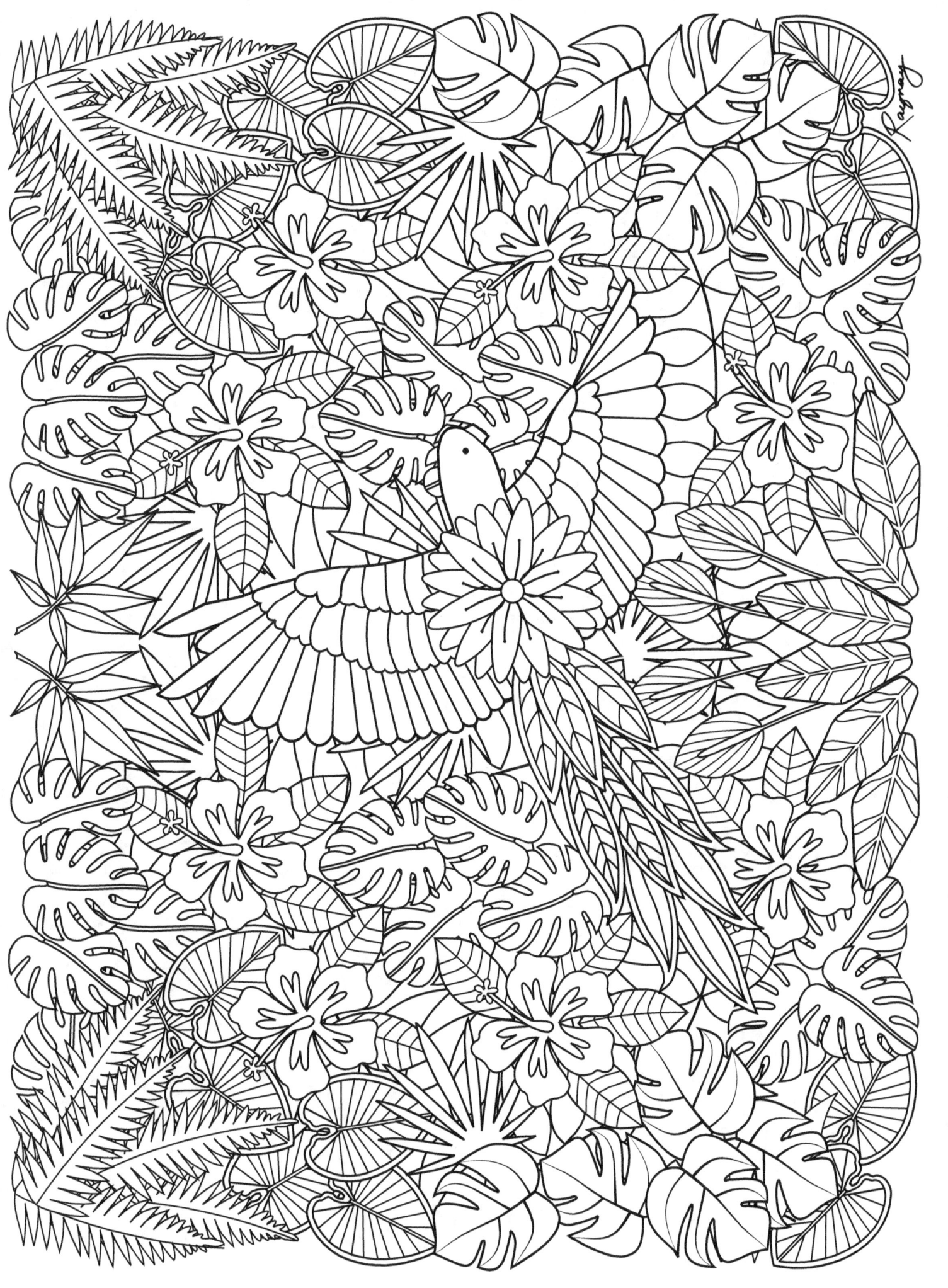

Title: The Swans

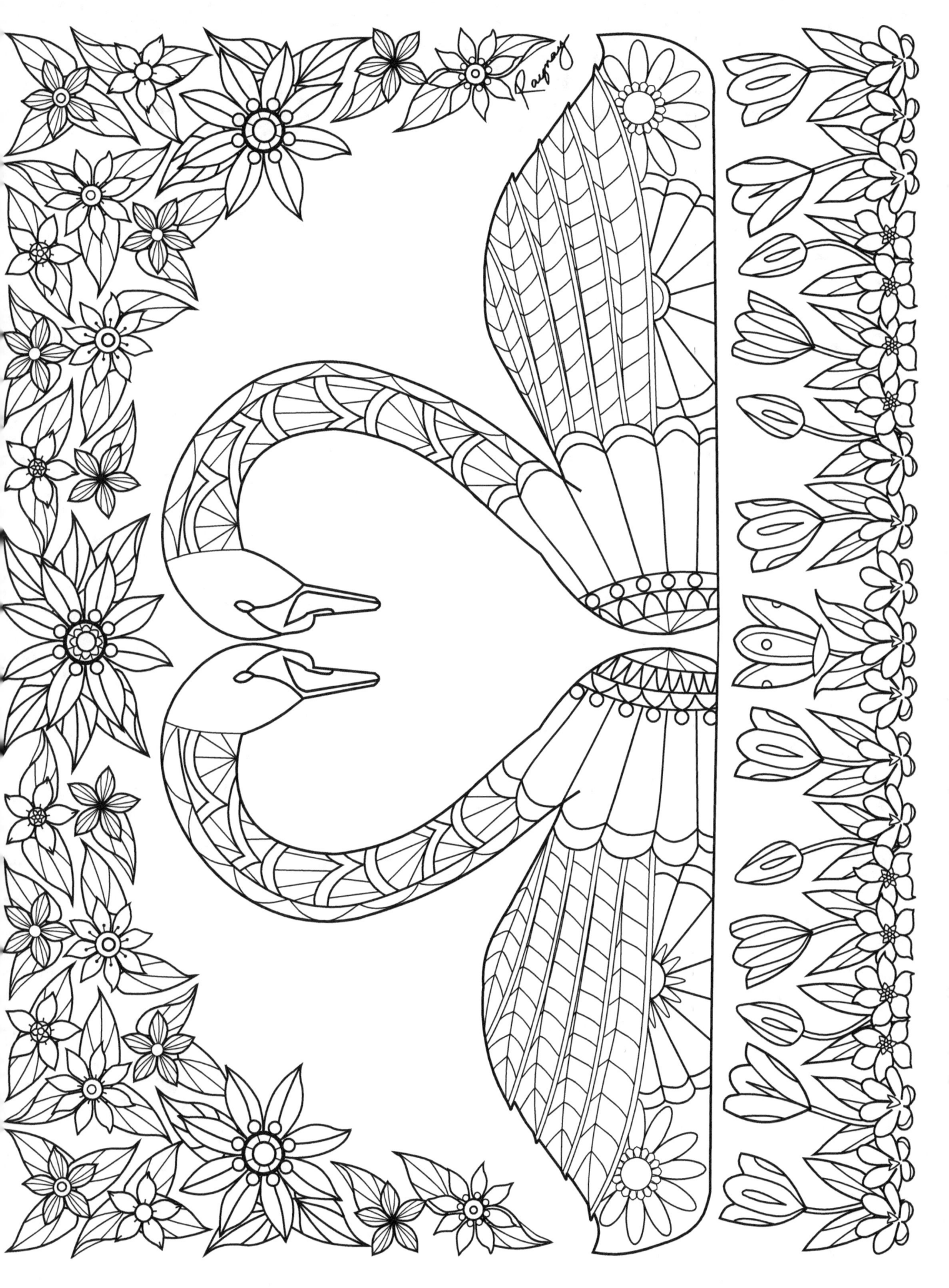

Title: Fox in the Shade

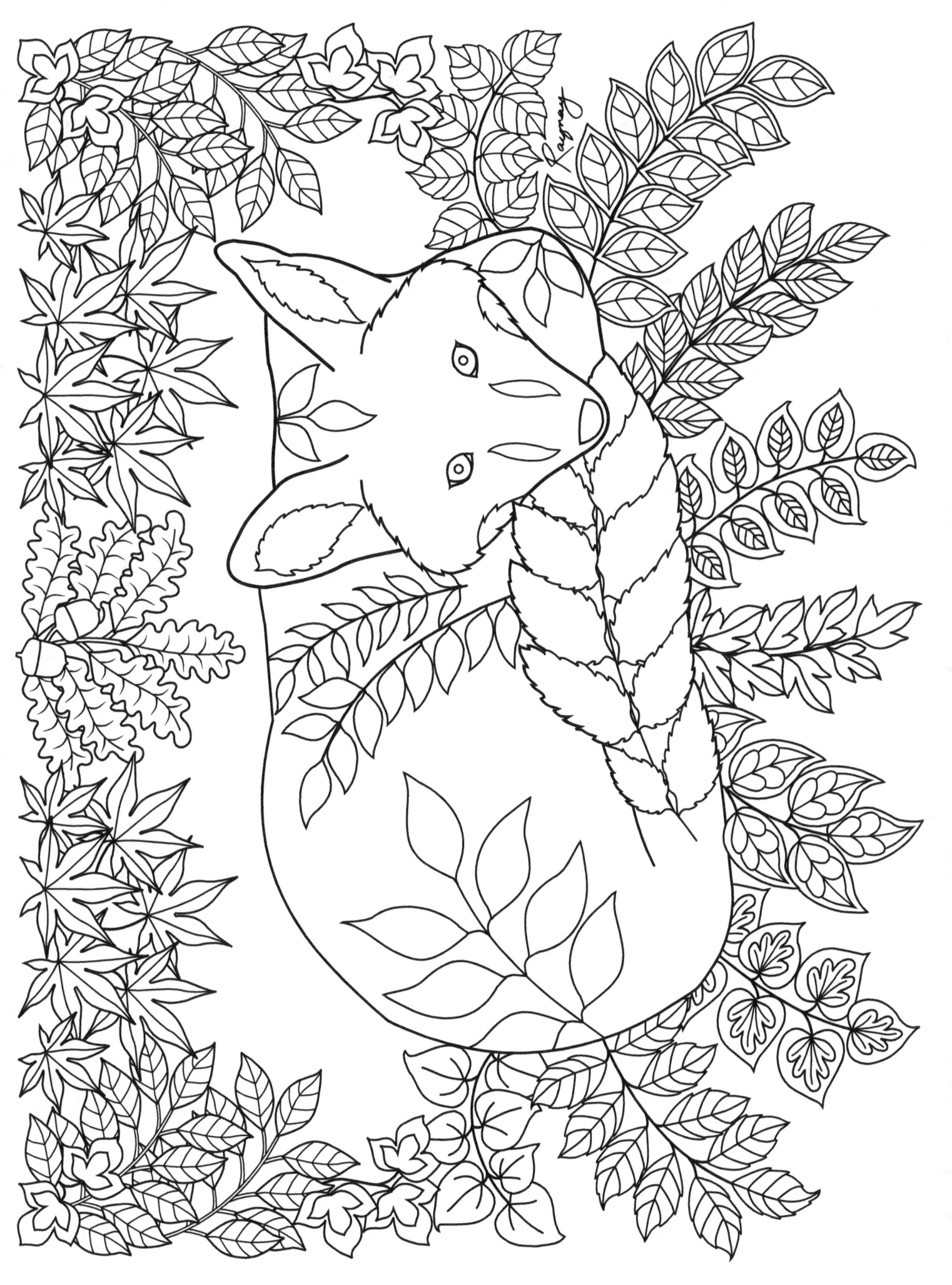

Title: Koi in a Pond

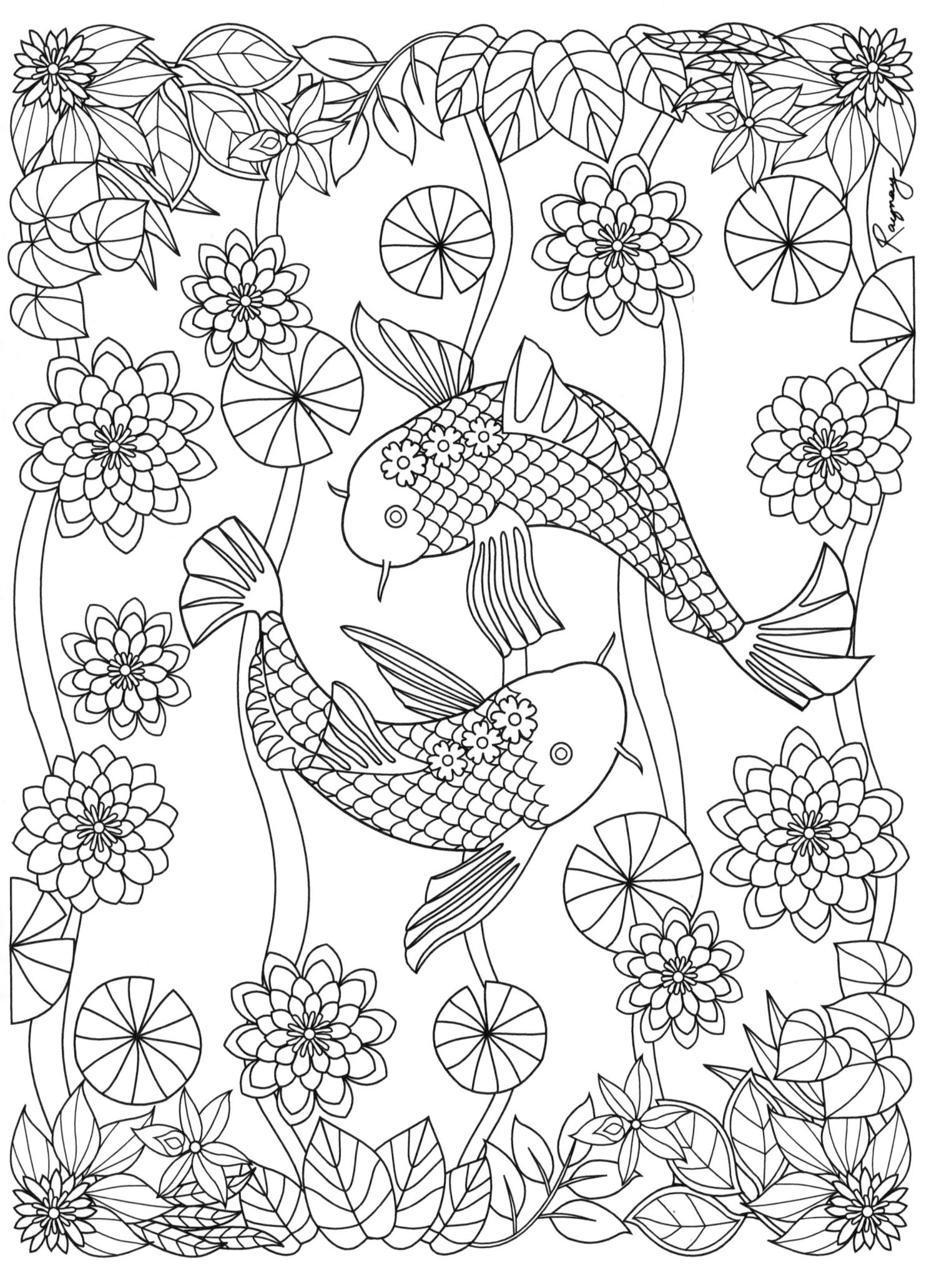

Title: The Flowering Shrub

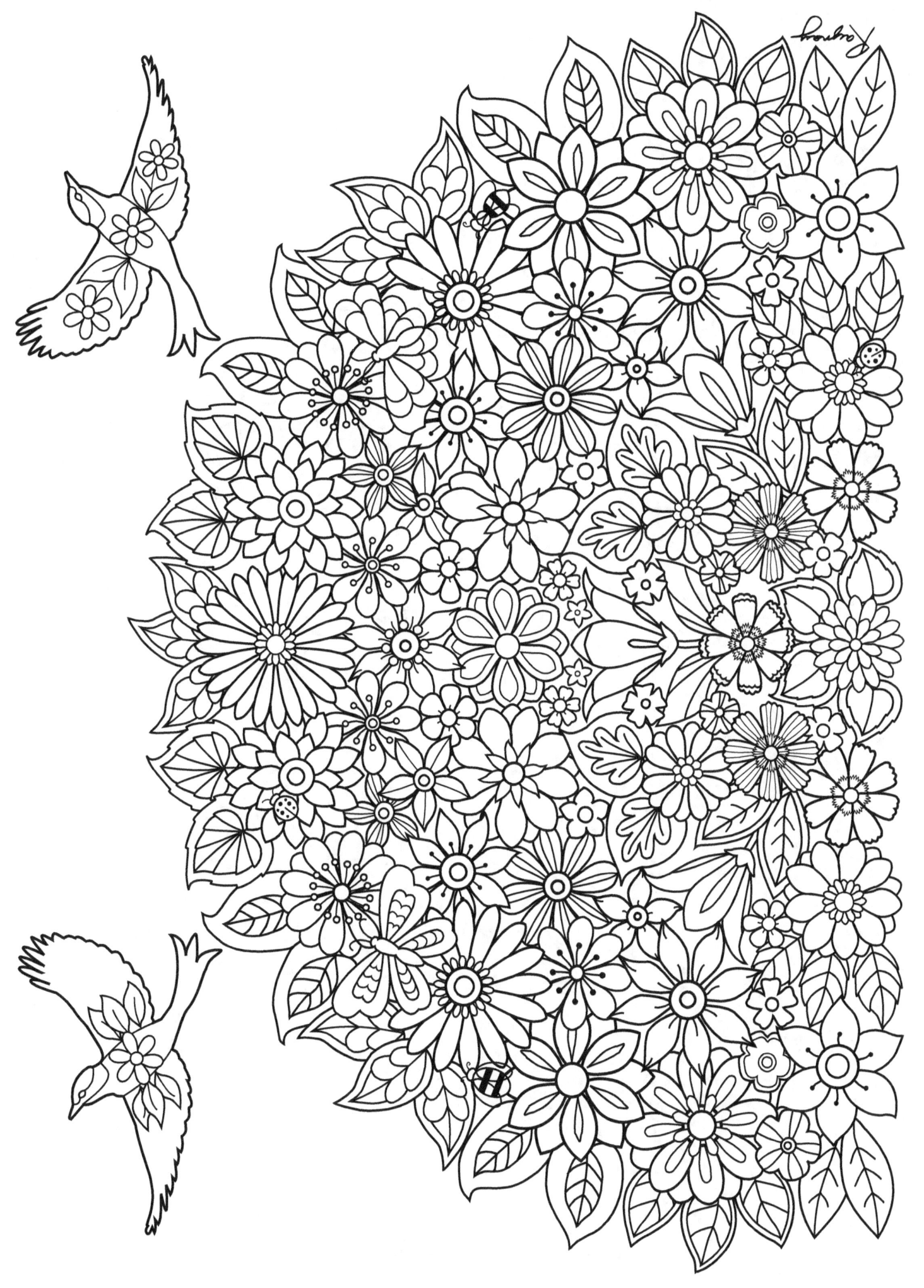

Title: Napping in the Garden

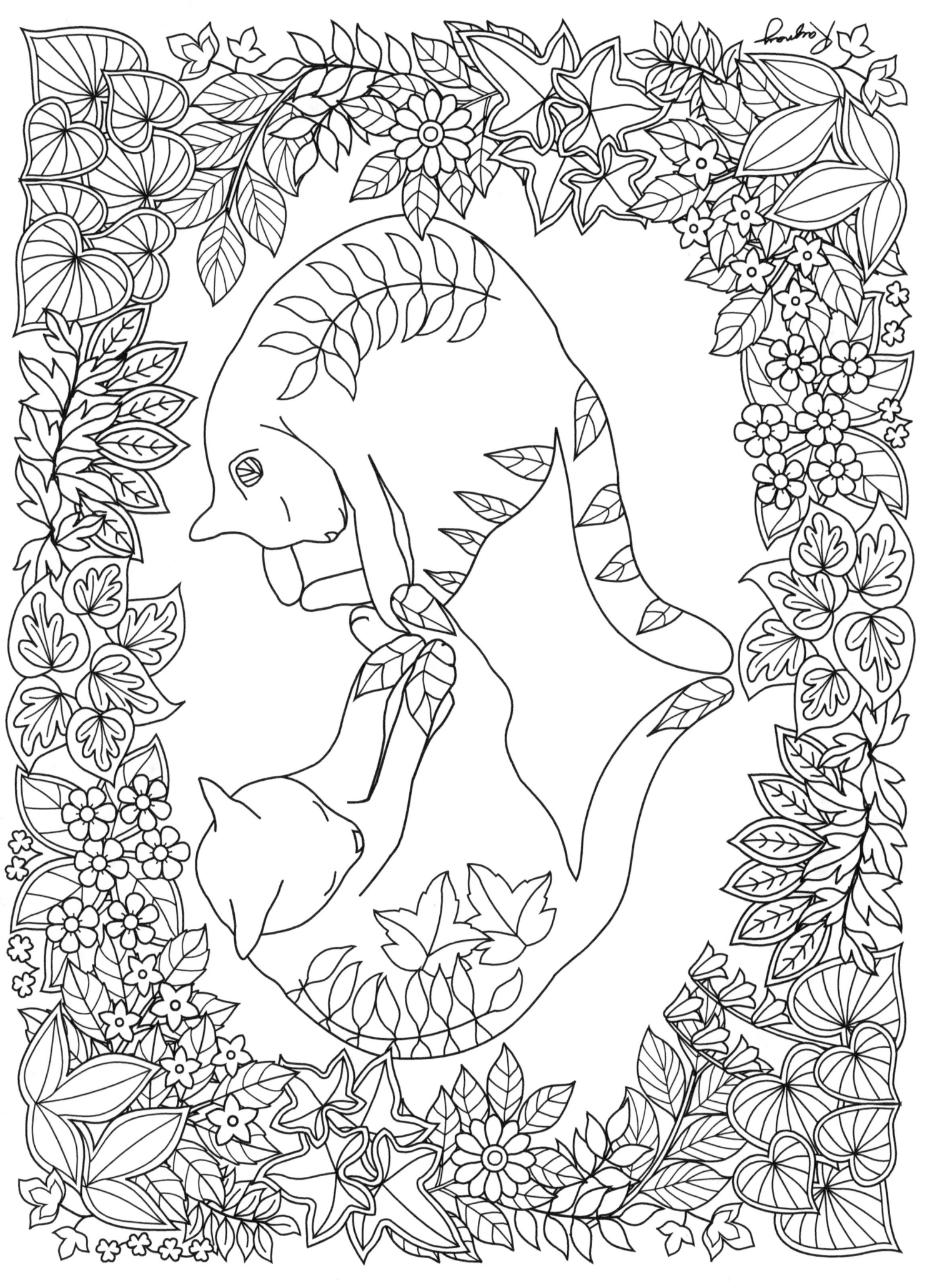

Title: The Butterfly

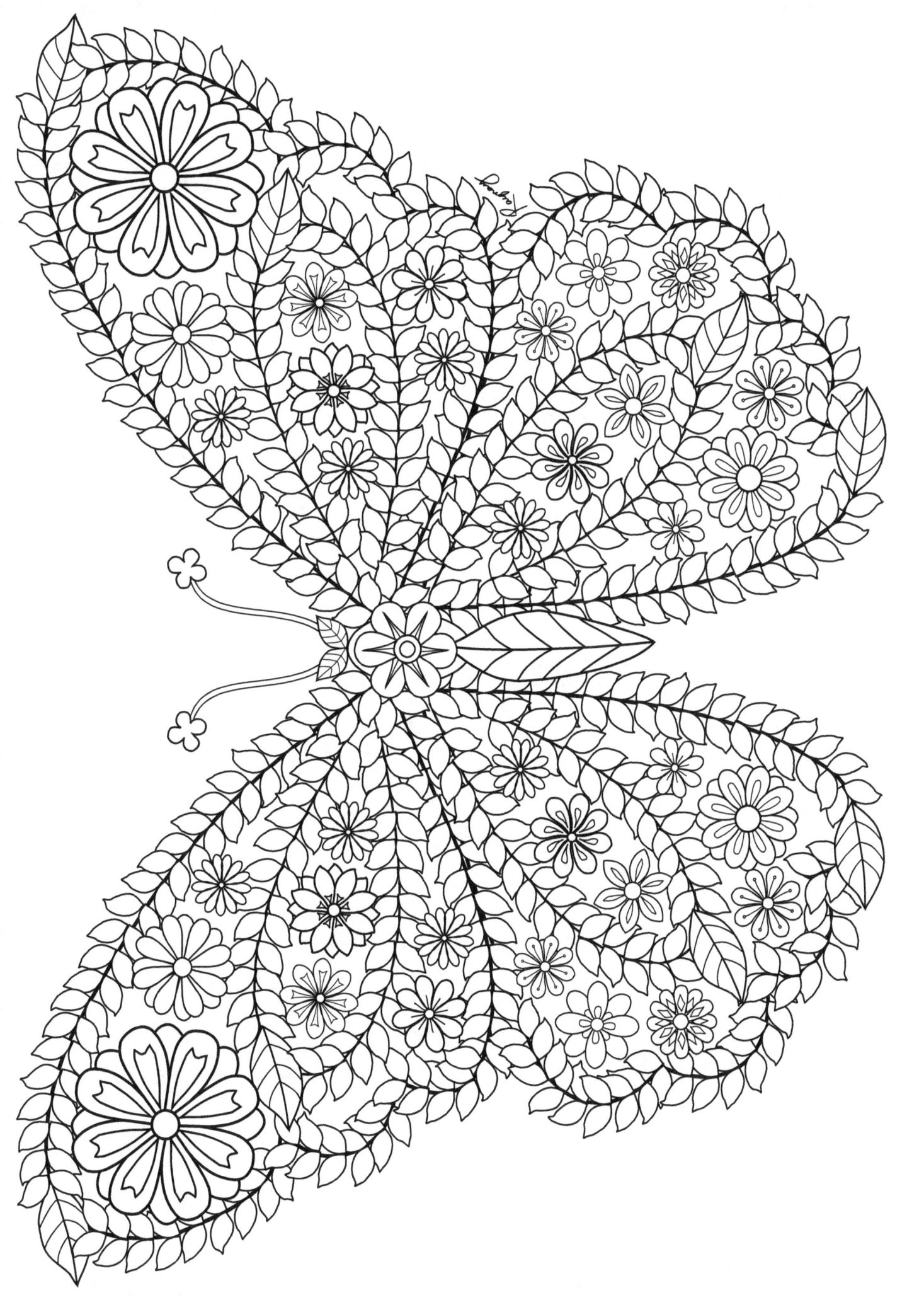